In a day when cultural forces are wreaking havoc on the church, the home, and the family, Keith Fournier's book is a much-needed antidote. He argues persuasively for the most profound of realities—that the home is a place of holy habitation.

Charles W. Colson
Author, Speaker, and
Chairman of Prison
Fellowship

BRINGING CHRIST'S PRESENCE INTO YOUR HOME

BRINGING CHRIST'S PRESENCE INTO YOUR HOME

Keith A. Fournier

THOMAS NELSON PUBLISHERS
Nashville

Published in Nashville, Tennessee, by Thomas Nelson, Inc., and distributed in Canada by Lawson Falle, Ltd., Cambridge, Ontario.

Unless otherwise noted, Scripture quotations are from the NEW AMERICAN BIBLE with Revised New Testament. Copyright © 1987 Thomas Nelson, Inc.,

Scripture quotations noted KJV are from the KING JAMES VERSION of the Bible.

Scripture quotations noted NKJV are from THE NEW KING JAMES VERSION. Copyright © 1979, 1980, 1982, Thomas Nelson, Inc., Publishers.

Scripture quotations noted NIV are from The Holy Bible: NEW INTERNATIONAL VERSION. Copyright © 1978 by the New York International Bible Society. Used by permission of Zondervan Bible Publishers.

Scripture quotations noted RSV are from the REVISED STANDARD VERSION of the Bible. Copyright © 1946, 1952, 1971, 1973 by the Division of Christian Education of the National Council of the Churches of Christ in the U.S.A. Used by permission.

Library of Congress Cataloging-in-Publication Data

Fournier, Keith A., 1954–
    Bringing Christ's presence into your home : your family as a domestic church / Keith A. Fournier.
    Includes bibliographical references.
    ISBN 0-8407-72223-8 (pbk.)
    1. Family—Religious life. I. Title.
BV4526.2.F64   1992
249—dc20   91-36920
                                                         CIP

Printed in the United States of America
1 2 3 4 5 6 7—96 95 94 93 92 91 92

This book is lovingly and admiringly dedicated to two men whose teaching on family life has significantly enabled, equipped, and empowered me to serve as a husband and a father: John Paul II and Dr. James Dobson. Their spiritual vision and practical insights are a great beacon in an otherwise darkening world. It is also, of course, dedicated to my own domestic church: my wonderful wife and friend, Laurine; and our congregation, Kristen, Keith, Ann, MaryEllen, and Joel.

CONTENTS

1

What Is the Family?

I woke up in church this morning. Not on a cold marble floor with the smell of votive candles in the air. Not in a bright sanctuary with a large pipe organ. Not in a church building however you may picture it. I woke up in my home, next to my partner in mission and ministry for fifteen years, my wife, Laurine. Down the hall were members of the "flock," Ann and MaryEllen, two of my daughters, and in the choir loft slept Kristen, Keith, and Joel, three more of my children. I was in church.

Now don't get me wrong. Church was not my house. I don't live in a section of a church building or in an adjoining appendage. I am not a minister or a priest. I am a lawyer. I am a husband and a father. The church I awoke in was not a building with beautiful stained-glass windows; it was, and is, my family. What a profound revelation this is for me. It sounds strange, doesn't it? How can I say that my family is a church? This concept is foreign to us because we often see church as a building where families gather with other families to worship, confess their sin, hear God's Word, receive the sacraments, serve the needs of others and pray.

These are wonderful activities. But "being church" is so much more than going to a building. The book of the Acts of the Apostles paints us a wonderful portrait of the way the early Christians understood their call to be church.

They devoted themselves to the teaching of the apostles and to the communal life, to the breaking of the bread and to the prayers. . . . All who believed were together and had all things in common; they would sell their property and possessions and divide them among all according to each one's need. Every day they devoted themselves to meeting together in the temple area and to breaking bread in their homes. They ate their meals with exultation and sincerity of heart, praising God and enjoying favor with all the people. And every day the Lord added to their number those who were being saved. (Acts 2:42, 44–47)

Look at the elements of the early Christian church in this passage: teaching, fellowship, breaking of bread, prayer, faith, common life, shared possessions, worship at the temple, praise, thanksgiving, witness of life, and mission. Often the reality of being the Church is confused with the action of going to a church building. The first Christians, as we see in this passage from Acts, did much more than pray together. Of course, attending the temple services was important to their community life. However, this was only one part of their experience of being the Church. Being the Church meant and still means being in a relationship of committed love with God and one another, being a community, being a family. The Christian church is fundamentally God's family.

Many of you are probably very much like me. If so, at first hearing, this message won't fall on immediately receptive ground. Yet it is such a vital part of the full gospel, the "good news," that we need to till the soil in order to receive it. These truths about the Christian family and the Church can and will deeply affect the way we live if we allow them to take root in the daily stuff of our family life.

Jesus speaks of the need to be fully open to the truth in His parable of the sower. One day, from a boat, He told His followers a story about a farmer:

A farmer went out to sow his seed. As he was scattering the

seed, some fell along the path, and the birds came and ate it up. Some fell on rocky places, where it did not have much soil. It sprang up quickly, because the soil was shallow. But when the sun came up, the plants were scorched, and they withered because they had no root. Other seed fell among thorns, which grew up and choked the plants. Still other seed fell on good soil, where it produced a crop—a hundred, sixty or thirty times what was sown. He who has ears, let him hear. (Matt. 13:3b-9 NIV)

The story has direct application to all who truly seek to live the full Christian message. The field is our heart, our mind, our life-style, and our capacity to hear and incarnate God's words. Too often the "birds" or predators of daily living sweep away the critical truths that can set us free.

For others of us, disappointments, failures, and pain so often associated with family life, render our hearts hard and unreceptive. We can hear truth and initially respond, but in the heat of the day, what we have heard does not find root deep within and our life-styles never really change.

Still for some, the thorns of doubt, fear, and mistrust simply squeeze the life and power right out of the truth of His Word before it has the time to transform us. Sometimes His Word will fall on rocks, thorns, and brush that have lodged there by the pain of a difficult natural family experience. Sociology and psychology experts tell us that more than 96 percent of American families today are somehow dysfunctional. I believe it.

We bring into our family life the accumulated experience of our own childhood. No wonder then that many of us find it extremely difficult to live a life-style where family becomes a domestic church experience. Yet we can find hope in those wonderful words spoken by the angel to the mother of Jesus, "Nothing is impossible with God" (Luke 1:37 NIV). We need to rediscover the truth about Christian family living so that we can enter into our full inheritance. We want to be the fertile ground where the truth of family life takes root, blossoms, and yields a rich harvest.

What Is the Church?

Just as we need to explore the full truth of family more deeply, so too should we reexamine our understanding of the Church. Many of us have a limited view of church, seeing it primarily as functional and institutional. Certainly it must contain function and structure, but the church is primarily and fundamentally a people: you and me, the people of God, called out as God's family to love one another and bring the gospel to the nations.

The apostle Peter reminded the dispersed Christians of the early church: "You are a chosen people, a royal priesthood, a holy nation, a people belonging to God. . . . Once you were not a people, but now you are the people of God" (1 Peter 2:9–10 NIV). Leaders of my own church restated it profoundly in their historic document on the Church, simply reiterating the ancient Christian understanding:

> All men are called to belong to the new People of God. This
> people, therefore, whilst remaining one and only one, is to be
> spread throughout the whole world and to all ages in order that
> the design of God's will may be fulfilled. . . . The one People of
> God is accordingly present in all the nations of the earth, since its
> citizens, who are taken from all nations, are of a kingdom whose
> nature is not earthly but heavenly."[1]

Church is the people of God in relationship. This way of looking at church is meant not only for the community at large, but also for the smaller more intimate community of the family. In fact, the call of the Christian family is to be a miniature church, to reflect all of the things present in the larger church community. As the Christian family, being church is our vocation and identity. It affects who we are and what we do.

Domestic church is a beautifully descriptive term that I sincerely hope you will take to heart. The phrase has been used over the long history of the Christian church as a way to describe the domestic experience as it was meant to be: a daily experience of church and a moment-to-moment experience of Christ's presence. The concept of *domestic church,* the family as a miniature church, actually clarifies for us how we are called to live our family life as a worshiping, serving, and loving community deriving our strength from the one whose death gave us life. Yet, all too often our experience falls far short of this vision.

If we take seriously Jesus' words to His disciples that "where two or three are gathered together in my name, there am I in the midst of them" (Matt. 18:20), we realize that whenever we gather together as a family with Christ as our Head, He has promised to be with us.

What an opportunity we have in the family to experience that continual presence of Christ. After all, where do we gather together more often than in the family? Every day we awaken within the sanctuary of the Christian home. If we could only take every opportunity to respond to the grace of being the domestic church, our families could not only be transformed, but also become transforming agents in the world.

Perhaps we need to reconstruct our concept of church and of family so we can see it at its deepest reality: family as church and church as family. I hope by the end of this book you will believe more firmly that the domestic church is God's plan for the Christian family that He laid out for us in the Scriptures. In fact, humans did not invent the family as a sociological construct. Rather the Lord has gifted us with the structure of family. Family is a reflection of His creative nature, His love, and His eternal purpose for all who would come to Him through His Son, Jesus.

The Modern Family

Too often our experience as Christian families is ineffective or incomplete because either we do not understand this call to be a domestic church or we have no idea how to live it. The fullness of God's revelation to the family has frequently disintegrated into a partial vision that lacks power and life. Instead of families being committed communities of love, prayer, and service working together for the whole Church, we have become isolated units serving our personal needs. We have lost the sense of our calling to mission—being families centered in the Lord and being instruments for His whole Body. We have also lost the context for realizing this ideal.

But that's not all. Not only will our Christian witness become more effective when we rediscover this vision, but by living God's complete plan for marriage and family, we will experience the joy and peace we so desperately desire in this life. In other words, to the extent that we live wholly in God's plan for Christian family, to that extent will we reap the fruits of His promises to us as believers and as His Church. So why are we not living out this vision? The answer varies for each person.

Many simply do not yet understand the call. I pray this book kindles a new fire for family living by painting afresh God's portrait for His smallest expression of church life. Others have forgotten to allow the Master to be Lord of the manor, and they listen instead to the secular idea of marriage, which is in many cases distorted, incorrect, and incomplete. God planned and created the family. If He is not the source of strength in a marriage, the life between husband, wife, and children cannot endure the pressure of daily life in an imperfect world.

Many families love each other on the natural level, which is good, but it's not enough to produce the selflessness essential to harmony or to sustain the sacrifice that is unavoidable in the true call of Christian marriage and family. We need supernatural spiritual strength to overcome all the obstacles we face. Christ alone can provide the fuel to steer the domestic ship through frequently troubled waters—of diapers, discipline, disappointments, adolescence, loss, death, distance—and into the tranquil sea of fidelity, endurance, and stability.

If a Christian couple is not consumed with this kind of vision, they leave room for the enemy to steal the seed of God's plan. There is intense spiritual warfare in Christian family living. The domestic church is the first cell of the whole Body of Christ. No wonder the legions of hell seek to confuse, dissipate, plunder, and weaken this holy sanctuary. But God, the author of family life, has another way. He wants to create within *your* home a holy habitation and to fill *your* family experience with true unity, joy, and life. Remember, however, we have an enemy who is cunning and determined.

Satan's counterattack is to spawn dissension, separation, mistrust, and hopelessness. The tactics of the enemy have not changed—divide and conquer. But Jesus warned us that "if a house is divided against itself, that house will not be able to stand" (Mark 3:25). Look at the contemporary statistics to see how many families the enemy has attacked and shattered. Look at the frightening rate of divorce, abortion, suicide, the pervasive lack of commitment, exaltation of self, and loss of honor and respect in many families. Statistics are not all that different within the Christian church or without.

One of the most frequent and dangerous problems facing the family today is a lack of quality time spent together. But if we begin to see the family as church, we more easily understand the necessity of time together. There is no substitute. Our families are to be genuine Christian communities, yet we are often more committed to our careers, hobbies, athletics, or other people than to our spouses, children, parents, or siblings. Our lives can become filled with so much activity, much of it essentially good, that we no longer have time for each other. But as Christian husbands, wives, and children, we must again choose the Lord as the first priority and live fully in His family, the Church, through our participation in its most intimate expression, the domestic church. This is not a one-time decision but a continual choice. Made once, it must be made again and again.

In my own life, with five children, my wife and I must face this choice daily. Personally, years ago I experienced it in a life-changing way. I was twenty-one years old, and my wife and I were expecting our first child. Understandably, I was intensely focused on my career. I was in my last year of college, taking 21 hours a semester and working between 35 and 40 hours a week to "make ends meet." I wanted to be a good provider, a good husband, and a good father; I wanted to be a great instrument for the Lord; I wanted to do all that I could for His Church. I was young, zealous, idealistic, and action oriented.

Prior to marrying Laurine, I had begun my college career as a religious postulant for the Benedictines, a Catholic monastic order. I had envisioned myself preaching the gospel and sharing my faith in Christ as a Catholic priest. But the Lord had a different plan in store. Because of my desire for the Catholic priesthood, when I left the monastery, most of my college studies had been in philosophy and theology. Both were disciplines I thoroughly enjoyed. I still do.

However, I discerned that the Lord was not asking me to forsake marriage for the Kingdom (Matt. 19:12; 1 Cor. 7), a prerequisite for ordination in my church. Still, I intended to continue in His service. So when He brought Laurine to me and gave us the gift of the Sacrament of Marriage, I continued to pursue my degree in theology. "After all," I thought, "I will be a lay theologian and live a truly meaningful life. Marriage won't stand in my way."

So I threw myself into studies and into ministry as a layman. I wanted to "fully" serve God. I even prepared my application for graduate studies at a renowned theological school in Europe.

I wanted to go all out for God and serve the Church. Both of these were good motives, but my family life began to suffer because of them. I was living a dichotomy between my family commitments and my desire for Christian service. I would later come to see that my priorities and my idea of serving God were out of order. I didn't understand the vocation of domestic church living.

My lack of vision was a product of my pride as well as a shallow understanding of the call to marriage and family. I will never forget the day when, during prayer, I sensed a new freedom in my spirit. I felt the Lord impress upon me a deeper revelation of His purpose and my primary vocation. I did not hear an audible voice, but the words were impressed on my heart: "Keith, if you do nothing more than raise faithful children for me and love your wife, you will have contributed significantly to My Church." That was the beginning for me of a deeper understanding of family life as a call and a vehicle to serve God and His Church.

I began to see that my vocation was to live my life for Him in the domestic church of my family and that everything else I did had to flow from that foundational calling. All of the New Testament admonitions to married men who served as leaders began to take on new meaning (*i.e.*, 1 Tim. 3:2-13). The directions that a married man be a good husband and a good father, a good manager, and a man of upright character were not simply a matter of external witness, but rather internally cultivated and externally demonstrated qualifications for leadership.

I began to understand that it was precisely in loving his wife "as Christ loved the church" (Eph. 5:25) and fathering his children as God fathers His (Eph. 6:4; Col. 3:21; Heb. 12:9), that a family man learned how to serve in the broader Church. In fact, any service he undertook beyond the domestic church had to be an extension of his demonstrated service and love within his own domestic church. My wife began to see the same principle in her vocation as a Christian wife and mother.

I also began to see that what I did to earn a living was not all that important. That is not to say that some married people are not called to derive their income from ministry or theology, but I wasn't seeking to do that out of a genuine desire. I was seeking to prove something to myself and others. I wanted to prove that a Catholic Christian layman can be effectively involved in ministry *and* family life. Instead I discovered that Christian family *is* ministry—my first ministry and a foundational ministry for all of God's people.

Furthermore, I discovered how difficult it was, at least for me, to make an adequate income with degrees in philosophy and theology. So, I asked myself what I wanted to do and what I had the natural ability to do well. It was obvious: I wanted to be a lawyer.

I will never forget the night I came home to my wife, Laurine, having decided to pursue law school. The excitement within me made it nearly impossible to sleep. The final time I looked at the clock it was 1:00 A.M. I made such a commotion that I awakened her. She was eight months pregnant and was not having an easy time sleeping. She looked at me as if to say, "What is the matter with you?"

"Honey," I said, "I want to go to law school. I've realized that my first call in serving the Lord is to love you and our children, and my priority is to provide for my family. Family life is my vocation, my response to God's call."

Most women at this point would have justifiably hollered at their husbands. But Laurine focused her heavy eyes and said, "Honey, I think that sounds like the Lord. I'll stand with you. Now go to sleep."

And over the years, she has stood with me through five children, sleepless nights, joys, sorrows, struggles, and victories. What I grabbed onto at twenty-one years old, I have held onto like a dog with a bone.

Yet over the years, sustaining this vision has been difficult. It is more convenient to opt for something that requires less work, less sacrifice. There are many other "family models" being offered. Some better than others. But most are inadequate.

I believe that one inadequate model of marriage and family is the modern concept of the "nuclear family," too often embraced by Christian families and doggedly protected. Yet one negative effect of this model can be an unfulfilling and limited family experience that can actually impede our ability to live the true call of family as domestic church. Yes, we are first and foremost, after our commitment to Christ, committed to our spouse and children. But that is only the beginning of our Christian family.

The family that Christian tradition speaks of was not a modern nuclear family with Mom and Dad and the statistical 2.3 children, but an entire extended family that brought within its circle of love aunts, uncles, grandparents, nephews, nieces, and even went beyond to embrace the local community of believers. This experience of family was at the heart of the early Christian church and helped pump the vitality of renewal through its veins. It can again if we rediscover its wealth and live it.

Like many of you, I come from a splintered natural family. The mobility of the contemporary age, the struggles of coping with fractured relationships, and the pain of struggle have left my natural family separated both by miles and, sadly, convictions. Though I still stay in touch with my parents, brothers, and sister, our contact is sporadic and limited by distance. Moreover, my experience of extended family is virtually nonexistent.

In the early church, the spiritual built upon the natural and as we will discuss later, the gospel found a home in a natural environment where extended family relationships were strong. One day when Jesus was ministering inside a building to a crowd, someone told him that his mother and extended family were outside. What He said has profound implications for us:

> He replied to him, "Who is my mother, and who are my brothers?" Pointing to his disciples, he said, "Here are my mother and my brothers. For whoever does the will of my Father in heaven is my brother and sister and mother." (Matt. 12:48–50 NIV)

We are all brothers and sisters of Christ, full members of God's family. No matter what our experience of natural family relationships, Jesus desires to supplement, restore, and rebuild it. He offers eternal family life with Him to those who come to the Father through Him. We are now joined by bonds of love that can't be broken. Bonds forged in the blood of the cross.

The problems facing families today are symptomatic of a deeper, underlying loss, the loss of a full understanding of the vocation of Christian marriage and family life. Until my family and yours embrace the vocation of our Christian family as a faith community that shares love, sacrifice, prayer, play, pain, and mission—until we become a domestic church—we will not realize our fullest potential or experience the depth of the gift given to us.

Partial visions, no matter how understandable or well-intended, will not endure because they lack those qualities that come only from being a domestic church with Jesus Christ as the cornerstone: constancy, stability, and strength. We need to re-capture and rebuild the full truth of the Christian family as the domestic church.

We need to restore the complete vision of a dynamic Christian family life. In the book of Proverbs, we read, "Where there is no vision, the people perish" (Prov. 29:18 KJV). Without a restored vision, Christian family life will be further damaged and weakened, but with this vision, it can be restored, renewed, and revived. In fact, it can become again the very seed that renews the contemporary church and eventually transforms our secularized culture. All of this may sound like the impossible dream, but I assure you it is not. Rather, it can be a reality. We simply need to rediscover our heritage as a domestic church and our place in the family of families, the universal Church.

A story is told of a beggar in an ancient land, a man who had become intensely bitter because of the deprivations of his life. He stood outside the city gate, never coming in, day after day, year after year, begging for food to fill his swollen and distended stomach. One day word spread through that land that the King was near death and that he had no heir to his throne but a son born twenty-five years ago who had been stolen, perhaps killed, by an invading enemy army. How the King longed to find his lost son. It was his last hope to continue his royal lineage.

The beggar heard the tale but thought to himself, "What does it matter to me? I am a beggar. I always have been and always will be. I have grown up alone in the desert and I will die alone in the desert."

A summons went out throughout the land to find the King's lost son. Couriers went into every city to search for Him. Such a courier passed by the beggar one day at the city gate. He threw a coin into his ragged sack, glanced at his forlorn face, and rode on. That night he recalled that face, worn by the ravages of loneliness. "Of course," he thought, "it is he, the King's son." The courier remembered noticing the strawberry mark on the right cheek of the beggar, the distinctive birthmark of the King's son.

Immediately he set out to find the beggar. When he did, he

dismounted his horse, threw his arms around him, and shouted for joy. The beggar was understandably frightened and resisted the messenger's efforts. In fact he had to be tied to the back of a horse and escorted back to the palace against his will.

Only months later did the unbelief, founded on loneliness and a lack of identity, give way to a recognition within the beggar of his royalty, his nobility, and his rightful place at the table of the King.

Well, you and I are that beggar. So many times, our experiences, disappointments, and lack of knowledge of the fullness of our relationship with God have rendered us beggars, collecting only the scraps of our inheritance. It's time to come into our full inheritance. We belong to the King of kings. We are part of His extended family, and our own households can become His palaces.

At this point, some may say, "Sounds great, but we're just one family. How can we live this vision alone?" You can't. But renewal always begins in small numbers. One family links arms with another and then another and, before long, a vast army has assembled.

But even as a small family we need not fear. We should take to heart Jesus' promise in Matthew 16:18: The gates of hell will not prevail against the church. If the Christian family is the domestic church, the gates of hell will not prevail against it. After two thousand years, the domestic church of the Christian family has endured. The gates of hell have not prevailed against it yet, and they won't if it remains firmly rooted in God's love, operating according to His plan, empowered by His Spirit and planted firmly within His Church.

All of this really requires a fresh new way of thinking. If we are serious about being what God desires us to be as Christian families, we need His vision and His plan. We need what St. Paul calls a "renewal of your mind" (Rom. 12:2). If we can capture again the reality of the Christian family as a miniature church, we will better understand the resources we have at our disposal to fight back the increasing attacks against a truly Christian family life. Furthermore, we will not only be able to defend our own family, but actually go on the offensive and once again see Christian families become the missionary shock troops that will bring revival to the church of the twenty-first century.

Rebuild the Domestic Church

We need to look again to the New Testament age and the apostolic age to rediscover an important truth about the structure of the Church. The structure of the Church grew out of the need and the experience of the people. The early believers gathered together first in the home (Acts 2:46) and then in larger groups. They related to one another first as brothers and sisters within the family, and then they began to organize. I believe that organization and structure is a gift from God, but nonetheless, we need to see the proper order of events. Family was first church; church then became a structured family of families. Semantics alone? No, a key to rediscovering our heritage and perhaps a key to true Church renewal.

We need to return to the original vision, to rebuild our understanding of the Christian family before we can rebuild the larger Christian church. Instead of just living in the world as families who happen to be Christians, we need to embrace again the vocation of being a domestic church and truly start daily living in church. We are no longer citizens of this world but rather citizens of God's household (Eph. 2:19).

I have always taken St. Francis of Assisi as one of my great inspirations. Heralded and appreciated by Christians of all traditions, Francis is a great example of a rebuilder. Shortly after his conversion, while praying before a cross at the church of San Damiano, Francis heard the Lord speak to him. The Lord said, "Francis, go and rebuild my church, which, as you see, is falling down in ruins around you."

At first, Francis thought the Voice that spoke to him was telling him to literally rebuild the falling chapels that cluttered the landscape of his day. And so he did. Only upon later reflection did he come to understand that the church he was called to to rebuild was alive, made of "living stones . . . being built into a spiritual house" (1 Peter 2:5 NIV). So it is today.

Like St. Francis, we face a decline of the domestic church and indeed the whole Church in our times. Our spiritual homes need rebuilding. Those living stones that Peter speaks of can also be seen as Christian families. We are the living stones called to rebuild the Church. If we are to rebuild the whole Church, we need to begin at home. We can no longer stand in weakened structures, feebly defending the onslaught of the enemy. We need to stand in the strength of our domestic churches, linked arm in arm, and watch him cower in our presence.

In addressing challenges faced by the early Christians in the Corinthian community, Paul reminded them of some critical building principles:

> Each one must be careful how he builds upon itm for no one can lay a foundation other than the one that is there, namely, Jesus Christ. If anyone builds on this foundation with gold, silver, precious stones, wood, hay, or straw, the work of each will come to light, for the Day will disclose it. It will be revealed with fire, and the fire [itself] will test the quality of each one's work. If the work stands that someone built upon the foundation, that person will receive a wage. But if someone's work is burned up, that one will suffer loss. (1 Cor. 3:10–15a)

Similarly we need to be careful how we rebuild the Christian family. Not only do we need the right blueprint; we need the right materials. Far too often we have used the wood, hay, and straw of some new (even well-intended), novel approaches instead of the precious stone and gold that has endured the challenge of all the ages. Rather than living out a truly Christian vision of family life, we have settled for a nice sociological notion buttressed with spiritual jargon. But the fruits of our error are frighteningly evident. We must return again to the foundation of Jesus Christ, the building principles given to us in the Scriptures, and the indestructible materials found within the confines of His Church.

These alone that have stood the test of time and been found to be ever fresh and sufficient in each culture and each age.

We need to also remember, however, that it is the Lord who does the building, and "unless the LORD build the house, they labor in vain who build it" (Ps. 127:1). No mere human strategy will rebuild the Christian family. Only a return to God's original blueprint will accomplish this task.

There is much work to be done. Let's garner the wisdom of the Scriptures and be like the master builder that Jesus tells us about in Luke's Gospel who first sets out the materials before building the tower:

> Which of you wishing to construct a tower does not first sit down and calculate the cost to see if there is enough for its completion? Otherwise, after laying the foundation and finding himself unable to finish the work the onlookers should laugh at him and say, "This one began to build but did not have the resources to finish." (Luke 14:28–30)

To rebuild Christian family life, we can't do it partially. We must use materials that will endure the test of fire, struggle, brokenness. We cannot build a nice shell that will collapse after the first strong wind. We must build on the cornerstone who is Christ and build on the apostolic foundation and wisdom of two thousand years of our extended family history.

We must begin by seeing that tomorrow morning, we will indeed wake up in church. If God's plan is for my family and yours to be a domestic church then let us rise to the occasion. The challenge is clear; let's begin together reconstructing the house. Let's begin by looking at the first Family, the Trinity, three persons in One God. A mystery, yes, but one that can lead us closer to an understanding of our own call to be the domestic church.

2

God Is Family

"Keith, when are you going to stop living in the world and going to church? I want you to live in the church and change the world."

Although these words were not audible, they rang in my ears louder than any spoken words ever could. They came to me during prayer, imprinting themselves on my mind and heart. I meditated on them . . . wrestled with them. They challenged me deeply, where I lived, where I had committed myself. They told me that I was going the wrong way, despite my sincerity. As a husband and father, God's plan for me began where He had placed me, in the heart of my family, not in my local parish, not on a street corner preaching Christ, not in a law office defending the needy, not even in a Catholic university spearheading evangelistic efforts on campus and in the surrounding community. The Lord called me to minister first to my family—my wife and children. Other ministry opportunities would come, and as time and other resources allowed, I could get involved in those. But He wanted me to know that regardless of what else I did, service begins at home—in my domestic church. The rest is overflow.

Over the years, God has reaffirmed this truth to me in countless ways. Among them was through a scriptural study that helped me understand three amazing truths:

1. God is family.
2. God is for the family.
3. God is our family model.

These truths are foundational to a clear understanding of domestic church.

God Is Family

The Bible reveals a great deal about God. It tells us, for example, that He knows all things, past, present, and future. It tells us He can do all that does not contradict His nature. We also learn from Scripture that God has always existed—that no one created Him, although He is the creator of all things. The truths about Him are innumerable, but perhaps none are more intriguing, more revealing, more relevant for our lives than the truth that He is family.

Scripture teaches and the church fathers have repeatedly confessed that God is one in nature but three in persons. He is the one and only God, as Isaiah the prophet so clearly reveals: "There is no God apart from me,/ a righteous God and a Savior;/ there is none but me" (Isa. 45:21 NIV). But He is also three distinct persons—Father, Son, and Holy Spirit (Matt. 28:19; Acts 1:1–5; Heb. 1:1–3). These three persons have always existed; there was never a time that the Father was and the Son or Holy Spirit was not. They are a coeternal community of persons in relationship, a divine, supernatural family living and loving in complete unity.

I use the word *family* because God reveals Himself in family terminology. For example, God refers to Himself as "Father." The Greek words used within many New Testament passages for "father" *(patir)* and for "family" *(patria)* derive from a similar root word. The words are close, not by accident of language, but because of the intended intimate connection between a father and his family. Many in our contemporary age have not seen or experienced this intimacy. This may be tragic, but we cannot abandon the truth of God's revelation.

In the second chapter of Paul's letter to the Ephesians, he tells us all, "Consequently, you are no longer foreigners and aliens, but fellow citizens with God's people and members of God's household, built on the foundation of the apostles and prophets, with Christ Jesus himself as the chief cornerstone" (Eph. 2:19-20 NIV).

Family is not our idea; it is not some sociological or relational notion we have invented. Rather, it is an expression of God's nature; it reveals the depth of personal relationship between the members of the Godhead. The Father loves the Son as His Son, and the Son loves the Father as His Father, and the Holy Spirit loves both the Father and the Son and is loved by both as the Spirit of love between them. Perfect harmony united in love. That's the unbreakable familial bond between God the Father, God the Son, and God the Holy Spirit.

God Is for the Family

Not only is God family in His essence—a Trinity in complete and perfect unity—but He loves human families, who reflect this mystery. He has proven through history how devoted He is to the family unit. Even a brief walk through some of the highlights of Scripture verifies this. But before we put on our walking shoes and start through the pages of Holy Scripture, we need to grasp what marks every family, even every individual. For it is this mark—this divine stamp—that makes us who we are and unites us with one another and with God. Even in our brokenness, we are the image of God.

His Image, Our Nature

Beginning at the beginning, we can see in the creation account the start of God revealing Himself as family and creating for His glory the first human couple. "Then God said: 'Let *us* make man in *our* image, after *our* likeness" (Gen. 1:26, emphasis added). Notice that in this account of creation, God uses the plural when referring to Himself. Throughout church history, Christian leaders, teachers, and sages have pointed back to this passage as unveiling the plurality of persons in the Godhead. Although it does not specify that God is triune, we know from other biblical texts that this passage must be referring to the Father, Son, and Holy Spirit, declaring their unanimous decision to make human beings in the image of deity. Of what would this image consist? What would characterize it? The meaning of *image* and the verses that follow in Genesis 1 and 2 make it clear.

The Reflection in the Mirror

The word *image* is a translation of the Hebrew word *eikon*, from which we get our word *icon*. Just as an icon of Joseph, Mary, or the apostle Peter stands for them without being identical with them, so we stand for God without being deity ourselves. But unlike statues or paintings, we are living, breathing icons. And we create living icons or images. We call them our sons and daughters. Though we are not them and they are not us, they represent us and reveal us to others. When people see my children, they see some of me in them—and sometimes that's scary, even to me! Sometimes they get a glimpse of my smile, my sense of humor, or even my perfectionistic tendencies. For good or ill, our kids are reflections of us. The same is true of us in relationship to God.

We are living, visible images of the living, invisible God. We may not be able to see the Lord with our physical eyes, but we can see Him in ourselves whenever we encounter something good. Some of these good traits are mentioned specifically in Genesis 1 and 2.

For example, the divine image in us includes male and female: "God created man in his image;/ in the divine image he created him;/ *male and female* he created them" (Gen. 1:27, emphasis added). This does not mean that God is male and female, anymore than it means that God has physical parts or sex organs. After all, *image* has to do with reflecting, revealing, and representing, not with identification. But it does mean, however, that men and women are visible, physical representations of the invisible, spiritual God. What makes a man a man and a woman a woman somehow mirrors deity. Without launching into an exhaustive treatise on this subject, we know that our sexuality distinguishes us from each other as well as uniting us. Men and women have different sexual organs as well as different sexual drives and needs, and yet these differences are best satisfied in the sexual union of a man and woman in the intimacy fostered by a loving marriage relationship. This sexual union is both recreative and procreative—it brings pleasure and product, good fruits from a good tree. And in this creative union of man and woman, the divine image glows brightest and even reproduces itself through children.

Yes, the man and woman are images of God separately, but they best exemplify His image together as procreators, creating images of Him out of their mutual intimacy. This is God's plan for His creation. And lest we miss it, God declared it to be so after He created Adam and Eve: "For this reason a man will leave his father and mother and be united to his wife, and they will become one flesh" (Gen. 2:24 NIV).

Now notice something else: it takes more than one image-bearer to create another image-bearer. Man and woman join together to create a son or daughter. They are both charged by God to "be fruitful, and multiply" (1:28 KJV). They can't create without the involvement of each other in the process. What is true on the human side is true on the divine side. Remember, the scriptural text says "Let *us* make man in *our* image." All the members of the Godhead were involved in the creative process, and not just with the creation of man but also with the creation of the rest of the universe (Gen. 1:2; John 1:1–3;).

Furthermore, we are image-bearers of God because we are created as communal or social beings. The image includes male and female, both of whom are called to join forces to populate and rule over the earth (Gen.1:26, 28). This would be impossible if we were made to be independent islands, with no need or desire for each other. But just as God is a harmonious community of three Persons loving one another and ruling over creation with a loving hand, so we were created to be a community of persons who would love one another unconditionally and unashamedly and rule over the earth with care. "Love your neighbor as yourself" is one of the two greatest commandments for a reason. Without a healthy dependence upon and support of each other, we cannot find relational, much less self-fulfillment. We are made for each other, not to be loners. We are truly the family of man, bearing the image of the Family of God.

How important is this image? Well, it's important enough that the Old Testament established that to take the life of another human being was tantamount to snuffing out the divine image, which is an offense God takes quite seriously (Gen. 9:6). Second, it is so important that we are to keep our tongues under control so we don't use them to curse God's image (James 3:8-9). Third, it's so critical that God commanded us not to supplant it by worshiping false images (Exod. 20:4-6). As theologian Henri Blocher so aptly states:

> If mankind is the image, does not the prohibition of making images of God appear in a new light? God himself has placed his image in his cosmic sanctuary, and he wishes due homage to be paid to it by the service of mankind, the neighbour created in his image. And Christ joins the first and great commandment with the second which "is like it"—"You shall love the Lord your God . . . you shall love your neighbour"; surely the logic behind that is the likeness between God and his image.[1]

And finally God considers our image so important that He sent His Son to earth to redeem and restore it into its original glorious state. When we place our faith in Christ, we nail our old selves on His cross and begin to cloth ourselves with "the new self, which is being renewed, for knowledge, in the *image* of its creator. Here there is not Greek and Jew, circumcision and uncircumcision, barbarian, Scythian, slave, free; but Christ is all and in all" (Col. 3:10-11, emphasis added).

This divine image joins us together as the family of man, making us individually and collectively mirrors of the divine Family.

We reflect the three-in-one God, and He has made us to respond to Him as He does within Himself—in familial love. He knows that He has created us to find temporal completion with each other, and eternal completion with Him.

I have always loved reading Hasidic folklore and rabbinical tales. One of my favorite stories concerns the creation account. Three learned rabbis were discussing the book of Genesis. "Why," said one, "after each of the first five days did God say that what He created 'was good' but on the sixth day, after he created man, he did not say it was good?"

"Well," suggested the second, "perhaps it was because man is not good?"

"No," said the third, "he is the apple of God's eye. The word, my brothers, in our tongue is not really translated "good" but "complete." Man, unlike the land, the sea, the animals, and the birds is not complete. He has a higher destiny to fulfill."

And so he does. A man is not complete without a woman and a man and a woman are incomplete without God. We were made for one another and for God. In those marvelous words of St. Augustine, "Our hearts are restless, until they rest in Thee." We are made for fellowship, for family with each other and with God. God knew the perfection of His own family unity and desired that perfection for man, the crowning of His creation.

Tragically, however, our first parents moved away from this perfect union with God. Fortunately God did not move away from them or from us. As we ran to prostitute lovers, our heavenly Lover continued to pursue us, to search us out and woo us to Himself. The Holy Scriptures are the story of our running away from home and our Father running after us. They reveal the God who is for the family.

Some Family Portraits

With our first parents, everything started out well enough. In fact, the opening portrait is beautiful: "The man and his wife heard the sound of the LORD God as he was walking in the garden in the cool of the day" (Gen. 3:8 NIV). They walked with God. They enjoyed Him, learned from Him, laughed with Him, worked with Him. They were, after all, the crown of His creation and contained something of His life, His very breath (Gen. 2:7). But they eventually succumbed to the perennial temptation that still faces us all. They chose not to walk under God's authority. Instead, they chose to exalt themselves above Him—they strove to "be like God" (Gen. 3:4–5 NIV).

The consequences of that rebellion were devastating. Their original unity that reflected the unity of the Trinity was now marred. Their experience of fellowship, of walking with God, was warped by sin. And their spousal failure bore its evil fruit in their offspring, Cain, who became a son of rebellion.

Just as the good fruit of their original obedience was manifested in their son Abel, the bad fruit of their subsequent disobedience was reflected in their other son, Cain. And that rebellion, that first human sin, has left its mark on all of us who have come from their lineage. There is a bit of Cain and Abel in all of us, the tendency toward obedience and the tendency toward disobedience. As the Scriptures say, the sins of the fathers are all too often visited upon the children (Exod. 20:5; Ezek. 18:19ff). The failure of a husband and wife to maintain and cherish that bond of peaceful obedience to God, which must be a part of any godly family life, opens the door to Satan—our greatest enemy—and brings disunity to the entire family.

But even after Adam's and Eve's rebellion, so great was God's love for them and their kids that He continued to seek their fellowship. Abel responded appropriately as he gave to God the first fruit, the firstborn of his cattle. Cain, on the other hand, chose not to respond to God, but instead chose the way of self-centeredness, giving to God what was left over from his farming. It is not that God preferred beef over wheat. No, He was interested (and still is) in the heart. Abel's heart was given to God and won him the Lord's favor. Cain's heart was given first to Cain and merited God's anger, for our God is a jealous God (Exod. 20:5), and He must be first.

Reading further, we see that God's fatherly love for Cain continued, even despite Cain's self-centered rebellion. The Lord said to him, "Why are you angry? Why is your face downcast? If you do what is right, will you not be accepted? But if you do not do what is right, sin is crouching at your door; it desires to have you, but you must master it" (Gen. 4:6–7 NIV).

Unfortunately Cain chose not to master his sin and ignored God's tender fatherly advice. He killed his brother. The first occasion of sibling rivalry bore the fruit of death. The consequences for Cain's decision were awful. He was banished to the land of Nod (Gen. 4:16), a word that means wandering. He was destined for a life of alienation and emptiness. He was separated from the One who gives meaning and purpose to life. He was cut off from the family. Cain's existence became a type of living hell. Salvation is not just eternal life, but eternal belonging, being part of the family. In a certain sense, therefore, he was no more, because "God took him away" (Gen. 5:24 NIV).

But the Father kept pursuing the family of man, even when it went the way of Cain. Fueled by the forces of hell, the human race followed the deceiver. The Scriptures tell us: "The LORD saw how great man's wickedness on the earth had become, and that every inclination of the thoughts of his heart was only evil all the time. The LORD was grieved that he had made man on the earth, and his heart was filled with pain" (Gen. 6:5–6 NIV). And yet with one man, He could find pleasure—Noah.

Noah, a man after God's own heart, responded to the Lord in faith (Heb. 11:8) and built an ark as God had instructed him. Then the Lord said to Noah, "Go into the ark, you and your whole family, because I have found you righteous in this generation" (Gen. 7:1 NIV). God would protect this family and use their obedience to give the other families on earth a chance to find salvation from the great flood that was to come. But only Noah and his family listened, so only they were saved. Just as the sin of Adam was visited upon his offspring, so the obedience of Noah was extended toward his family. We who are parents must never forget this. Our response to God can have an eternal impact, not only on us, but our children as well. God sees us as families.

Another significant figure in our family history was Abraham, called with his family to be the father of many nations. Abraham is another classic portrait of faith held out to us in the New Testament letter to the Hebrews (Heb. 11:8ff). Abraham, like Adam, walked with God. He was a God's friend (2 Chron. 20:7; James 2:23) through faith. He said yes and God was able then to unleash his mercy and provision. Abraham became the Father of nations and his family a model of God's fidelity. His faith is heralded as the right response to the invitation of God. Those of us who follow the son of God, Jesus Christ, become sons of Abraham through faith (Rom. 4:3; Gal. 3:6).

What emerges in this brief walk through Scripture is the revelation of God's great love for us as family and a commentary on our various responses to His loving call. With the creation of our first parents, God intended a model of selfless love. Adam and Eve lived a life of fellowship where they walked with Him in the cool of the day. We see creation in harmony and unity because fellowship with God brings such traits. Yet, we see the act that precipitated the fall in Genesis 3 when we chose through the instrumentality of our first parents to be served rather than to serve, to be "god" rather than to be creature. And through our first mother, Eve, we cried out as a race, "We will not serve."

This act of rebellion flawed the image and original plan of God. Sin always does. Yet the desire for intimacy and fellowship was nestled deep in the Father's heart, His committed love that would not let us go. Through the flood and the ark of Noah, through Abraham and the Law, and through the judges and the prophets, He sought to communicate with us and teach us how to walk once again in His family way. But we continued to succumb to our own sin.

So "when the fullness of time had come" (Gal. 4:4–7), God sent forth His Word, the Son, to restore the image. God the Father sent His son for the salvation of the world! And how did He send Him? He was born into a human family. The unlimited God Himself was incarnated into our limited capacity and through that action removed our limitations, elevating us to a new level of relationship. God who is family expanded His family through the first born, Jesus Christ. Jesus became the bridge that brings us into a family relationship with God. With the birth of Jesus came the birth of the first New Testament church, the Holy Family of Nazareth. Joseph, Mary, and Jesus. They are the model that shows us the incredible connection between family and church. They are the fulfillment of all that was prefigured as family living in the Old Testament. We saw God loving the human family in the Old Testament; now we see Him entering that family in human form. Mary, fully human, is overshadowed by the Holy Spirit (Luke 1:35), and in fulfillment of all the promises of God gives birth to a Son who would become "The firstborn of a new creation." Jesus' whole Church, His whole family, would become the "new Israel," the family God had sought from the beginning. What a mystery! What a wonder!

Yet, although Jesus came to restore the original plan for the unity of man and woman and our fellowship with God, unfortunately, instead of communion, we often experience continual division in the family of God. Christ's love was required to undo the centuries and centuries of division brought about by our own sin and rebellion. It still is. Throughout our Lord's earthly ministry, His love would be the agent of unity and growth for the family, beginning with the twelve and extending to seventy-two and then to the whole world. He loved in all situations. He loved when He walked, laughed, wept, taught, fed, healed, relaxed, and celebrated. His self-giving love eventually led to the stretching out of His arms on the cross and now to a supernatural intimacy through the power of the Spirit with each believer and corporately with the Church.

In pursuit of family, Jesus set His eyes on the cross. He knew that it would be the bridge of restoration for a fallen human race, bringing it back to fellowship with a loving God, a God of covenant and family. To finish this task, He sent the Holy Spirit among us. His purpose—nothing less than to incorporate the church, through Him, into the very life of God at the end of time. The church is God's family, sons and daughters of the Father, brothers and sisters of the Son, and guided in those relationships through openness to the Holy Spirit, the active agent of God's love which transforms us and prepares us for the final family reunion in the life to come. That is why in the Revelation that majestic prayer concludes the whole Bible: "The Spirit and the bride say, 'Come!'" (Rev. 22:17 NIV). That is why the Church is described as the Bride of Christ. Family in all of its beauty and mystery is God's idea.

God Is Our Family Model

We are His image, His crowning creational achievement, the ones created to be in covenant love with Him. As such, we are called to model our lives after His. As individuals, as couples, as families, as brothers and sisters in the faith, the triune God is to be our model for loving, harmonious, community life. And when we look at Him, we find a divine Family who accepts us unconditionally and loves us covenantally. Let me show you what I mean.

Covenant Love

God has established an eternal relationship with us. He has given us a new and everlasting covenant. Our Lord is a God of covenant. We read of covenant fidelity in the Old Testament, and we experience it in the New. God's unconditional, committed love is part of His nature as family. His total fidelity makes Him the perfect model of spousal commitment and selfless love. Covenant love is the heart of Christian marriage, and therefore a proper understanding of covenant love is integral to a full understanding of Christian marriage and family life.

What is covenant love? The concept of covenant is much more than a legal contractual agreement. The Old Covenant was not simply God agreeing to be faithful and legally binding Himself to His promise. It was God being in love and acting in love. The covenant between God and His people was and is about a love relationship with His people. God's love affair with Israel is expressed in His covenant. He made a promise of fidelity and faithfulness that would never be broken even though it would eventually break His own heart.

The Old Testament is overflowing with examples of God's faithfulness to His promises. We see God's promise to our first parents, His promise to Abraham, His promise to Noah and his descendants, His promise to Moses and Joshua, His promise to David, and through the prophets, His promises to His people, Israel. And even though human beings were not and are still not faithful to God, He remained faithful to His part of the relationship. Many of the Old Testament stories demonstrate this. They show God reaching out to His children, even in their infidelity.

We see His gentle compassion revealed through Hosea, a prophet who was called to challenge Israel in their unfaithfulness but also to underscore God's unfailing love by prophetically demonstrating it for the people of Israel. You can almost hear God's fatherly heart breaking in the tender words of that great prophet:

> When Israel was a child I loved him, out of Egypt I called my son.
> The more I called them, the farther they went from me. . . .
> Yet it was I . . . who took them in my arms;
> I drew them with human cords, with bands of love;
> I fostered them like one who raises an infant to his cheeks;
> Yet, though I stooped to feed my child, they did not know that I was their healer. . . .
> How could I give you up, O Ephraim, or deliver you up, O Israel? . . .
> My heart is overwhelmed, my pity is stirred.
> I will not give vent to my blazing anger. . . .
> For I am God and not man, the Holy One present among you.
> (Hos. 11:1–4, 8–9)

God verbalized his pain through Hosea. Anyone who has ever experienced rejection or infidelity can relate to this pain. Unlike we humans, however, God never closes His heart. He always opens Himself for more love even at the risk of more pain.

Throughout the pages of the book of Hosea and indeed the whole Old Testament, God is revealed as Husband and Father, and Israel as bride and child—family life at its best! The imagery is inspiring but is more than simply a powerful metaphor. The language of family is fitting precisely because it captures God's revelation as family and His commitment to us. As family He mediates His love for us and to us. He offers us life in His very family.

Now as is the case in any mutual love relationship, response is key to the offering. So although we see God offering Himself to us continually, His intimacy and compassion are often met with human obstinacy and self-centeredness. The power of sin and rebellion impedes our ability to respond with fidelity to His covenant love. But God will not stop loving! That is what covenant is all about. He was and is faithful to His original plan of inviting the whole human race into His family.

Throughout the Old Testament we see this God of covenant love calling an entire nation to be His family. This is particularly evident in God's dealings with Moses. One of the Hebrew words used throughout the Old Testament that expresses the nature of covenant love is *hesed*. This word has no direct corollary in English because our language simply fails to grasp the profound depth of it. The closest words we have are *merciful* or *faithful love*. God demonstrated *hesed* love countless times in His dealings with Moses and the Hebrews. If anyone deserved abandonment, the Hebrews did. But their leader Moses, gifted with prophetic wisdom as to the very nature of God, stood on the fidelity of God. Amidst the gripes and complaints of the Israelites, Moses was able to cry out to God for mercy, not because the Israelites deserved it, but because he knew that God is mercifully faithful. Even more profoundly, God wants to reveal these truths to us. Look at what He revealed to Moses as he begged, "Show me your glory" (Exod. 33:18 NIV). God responds to Moses, "I will proclaim my name, the LORD. . . . I will have mercy on whom I will have mercy, and I will have compassion on whom I will have compassion" (Exod. 33:19 NIV).

In the New Testament, the apostle Paul, especially when writing to Timothy, reminds us of the enduring nature of God's fidelity. In the following verse, Paul reveals a profound truth about God's love for us: "If we are unfaithful/ he remains faithful,/ for he cannot deny himself" (2 Tim. 2:13).

When I hear this passage I often think of a close childhood friend who in a real way experienced the pain of denial. This friend was raised in a devout, orthodox Jewish home, but after a lengthy search for the truth, he embraced Jesus Christ as his Jewish Messiah. As a result of his choice to follow Christ, he was literally disowned by his family—no longer welcome in their home, no longer called "son." This degree of severity is at the heart of Paul's use of the word *deny* in 2 Timothy. Paul is telling us that for God to cease embracing us in His love would require a definitive act on our part of literally disowning Him. Second Timothy 2:13 shows us the wonders of God's affection as it tells us that even if we are faithless (and we all know our propensity toward that), He remains faithful. In other words, our continual sin, though it grieves His heart, will not stop God's fidelity because He is by nature faithful and so can never be unfaithful. As long as we who are in Christ Jesus continue to repent and to express our love to God, He can never deny us. We are part of Him, and He cannot deny or disown Himself. What a great source of hope for us!

Following Our God in Family Life

Given who God is and all He has created us to be and enjoy, we must look to Him as our perfect model for family life. For example, the relationship between husband and wife is to mirror the unity of God Himself, just as the relationship between Christians in His church is to reflect His unity (Eph. 5:31–32). As Christian married couples, we have the opportunity to participate in a creative union that imperfectly but beautifully reflects the fertile union of the Trinitarian God.

As human families, we of course fall short of this "perfect union." Often we fail to lay down our lives for one another in the

31

day-to-day grind. We distance ourselves from each other by arguing, being selfish, being insensitive, deceiving, not trusting, or hurting one another. We step out of union in so many ways, but we should never lose sight of the goal or become discouraged at our continual failure. Discouragement is a favorite tactic of the enemy to stunt our growth into holy families. Christian families, indeed Christians in general, should see themselves not as perfect but on the road to perfection. We are on the road to "becoming," growing into what God has revealed as the perfect model of Christian love. God, the "perfect family," is our first source of instruction and inspiration, but we can never be the "perfect family." Nonetheless, God continues to beckon us more deeply into His plan for family living.

Hope for Living

At this point you may feel overwhelmed. "How can my family be a domestic church? You don't know how weak I really am." Don't worry. There is One who possesses all the authority in heaven and on earth. He knows us better than we know ourselves. And in the words of the apostle Paul, His "power is made perfect in weakness" (2 Cor. 12:9). That is what we need—His power, the power of the Holy Spirit. Just as richly as He desires to lavish it on His whole church, He desires to lavish it on the church in your home. In the next chapter, we'll begin to see how.

3

Power for Family Living

The apostle Peter gives me great hope. He is a wonderful example of what it means to be fully human and fully in love with the Lord. Peter was nearby at most of the significant moments in Jesus' final years, and most of those times he responded in ways that were less than heroic. He was afraid to walk on the water; he doubted the miracle of the loaves and fishes; he tried to take control at the Transfiguration; he fell asleep in the garden; he denied Christ; he deserted Jesus at the cross. In most situations, Peter seemed impetuous and stubborn, yet also decisive, wholehearted, and sincere. Yes, though he put his foot in his mouth many times, he truly wanted to serve.

Peter's human condition seemed to get in his way. His need for quick answers, his desire to control, his insecurity—all of these things paralyzed him in the moments of great testing. Peter was a natural leader and a man of great strength. However, as strong as Peter was in the natural, he still failed the Lord. The same is true for us. Living only in the natural is not enough. Christians need supernatural power to combat the tremendous temptation to succumb to the fallen nature, to the "weak flesh" (Matt. 26:41).

The Lord has provided the strength for us. He has given us the ultimate source of supernatural power, the Holy Spirit. Peter received the power of the Holy Spirit, and look what happened to him! After the Spirit came upon him at Pentecost, he had the power to overcome his human fear. Driven by the Spirit of God, he confronted the crowds that once frightened him with the first public proclamation of the good news of Jesus Christ. Scripture says, "Peter stood up with the Eleven, raised his voice, and proclaimed to them, 'You who are Jews, indeed all of you staying in Jerusalem. Let this be known to you, and listen to my words.'" (Acts 2:14). Peter's first public sermon (obviously anointed by that new infusion of the Spirit) is one of the most compelling in the New Testament. He spoke with authority the full, uncompromising truth of the gospel of Christ. Three thousand people were converted that day because of Peter's response to God's holy gift.

It is a long-standing Christian tradition that this same Peter would stand faithfully for the Lord through terrible persecution and in the end, would go to Rome to be crucified for his Master. One story again has Peter seeking to escape Rome, but on the way out of the city, he is said to have seen the Lord walking into the same city. So, he turned around and went to his death, martyred for his love for Jesus. Yet another tradition tells us that Peter asked to be turned upside down when he was crucified because he felt unworthy to die in the same manner as his Master. Peter—an ordinary man who became extraordinary by the power of the Holy Spirit.

How is this pentecostal experience, this power, relevant for the Christian family? Well, just as Peter needed the power of the Spirit to lead the early church, we too need that power to answer God's call for our lives. Each one of us has a specific call, a Christian vocation. If we are called to the vocation of marriage and family—if we are called to build the church in the home—we, too, need spiritual power to live out that call. Peter's natural personal qualities would not have enabled him to fulfill such a tremendous position of leadership and service. Only the supernatural life flowing through him could do that.

Similarly many parents feel unequipped for the responsibility of leading their domestic church. We, too, need that "power from on high." In a special way, as pastors of the domestic church, parents should pray for a daily outpouring of the Holy Spirit for themselves and their children. Like Peter, if we are to be the instruments of change in the family, we need to seek and respond to the Holy Spirit. The same Spirit that transformed Peter can transform you and me and our families.

I have seen the reality of the Holy Spirit's gentle and gradual work in my own family over the years. But there have also been special moments of grace where the transformation has been particularly evident. I like to call these "mini-pentecosts." These are the times when God chooses to take the ordinary moments of daily life and transform them into extraordinary moments of grace.

One of these times was clearly a life-changing experience for my family. Several years ago my wife and I felt it was time to take the whole family through a basic refresher course in the Christian life. If you are anything like us, you know how easy it is to forget the basics. We chose the week before Pentecost. So every evening after dinner we would gather in the living room and discuss who Jesus was and what it meant to be a Christian. Our format was rather simple, consisting mainly of short presentations given by my wife and myself, most of them presented in a dialogue manner.

The sessions included vital areas of the basic Christian message including salvation, faith, prayer, perseverance, and a special focus on the power of the Holy Spirit. We invited some single men and women from our church who had become close to our family over the years and who shared a special relationship with our children. We planned the entire event to conclude on Saturday evening, Pentecost vigil, when we would attend the Pentecost services together.

Throughout the week I used two extremely helpful diagrams that were brought to particular prominence by Campus Crusade for Christ in the 1960s. Each diagram had a throne in the center. On one throne was a cross and on the other throne was an "E" standing for "Ego" or self. While preparing for these sessions, I was reminded of these words I once read: "In every man's heart there is a throne and a cross. If Christ is on the throne, then self should be on the cross. If self is on the throne, then Christ is still on the cross."

At the heart of this idea is the central command of Jesus Himself: "Whoever wishes to come after me must deny himself, take up his cross, and follow me" (see Matt. 16:24; Mark 8:34; Luke 9:23). The gospel is not first about self-fulfillment, but rather self-denial. It's true that a fruit of that self-denial is ultimate self-fulfillment, a powerful example of the paradox of the Cross and the whole Christian message.

As Pentecost week progressed, our children grew more and more engrossed in the discussions. One night I held up both of the diagrams and frankly asked everyone, "Who's on the throne of our lives?" Silence filled the air for what seemed an hour as we all wrestled with the reality of our own self-centeredness.

The first one to shatter the tension was my son, Keith. Children hold little back. Unlike "grown-ups," they have not yet learned how to conceal and control. "Dad," Keith said, "I think I'm still on the throne." After he broke the ice, we all ended up admitting the same thing. We also prayed together seeking the Lord's forgiveness and help.

My family came to understand something that night—that neither Keith nor any of the rest of us could have responded as we did were it not for the power of the Holy Spirit revealing the truth to us. This is one of the most powerful lessons we learned throughout our series, and I think it left an indelible impression on my family. We realized afresh that the apostles didn't have sole access to God's Holy Spirit; we do, too, and we desperately need it for daily family life. His work in our daily lives is to inspire, encourage, teach, correct, direct, empower, and equip us.

The crowning event of the week was the privilege of praying with one another to receive a fresh outpouring of the Holy Spirit. What we discovered, once again, is that life in the Spirit is an indispensable requirement to moving from self-centeredness to self*less*ness, from being a group of individuals to being the domestic church. If we are serious about a family life that reflects the life of God; if we are serious about being a church in miniature, we need the life of the Holy Spirit animating our every action.

As the years have passed since that event, so much has happened to complicate this simple truth. We now have the added burdens and changes (as well as the blessings) of a fifth child, teenage years, the aging process, relocation, and the other ordinary events that occur in every home. Things have not gotten easier, but that mini-Pentecost has been followed by other events of spiritual significance woven into the fabric of dailiness. Birthdays, sacraments, emergency rooms, family crises . . . all can become occasions for that desperately needed power that only God's Holy Spirit can bring. If only we will pray, the ordinary experience of family living can become quite extraordinary.

How does the Spirit actually change our daily lives in the family? He does for us what He did for the early church after the first Pentecost. Remember, there was a change in the daily experience of the apostles. There still can be. They had a new power and experienced a new sense of unity. So can we. Power and Unity—necessary for the universal Church, necessary for the domestic church.

Empowerment

The word that is translated as "power" in the biblical text is the Greek word *dunamis* from which we derive our word dynamite. God wants to give us dynamite power to be His church, to live the full gospel commission and to be Christian families. He wants us to be explosive in our witness to the gospel. There is a burst of energy when the Spirit of God touches the human spirit. That energy becomes a reservoir of power that constantly generates life within us. Fortunately we can tap into the power of the Holy Spirit through many vehicles. When we receive the holy Eucharist, and other sacraments, when we read His Word, when we pray with one another, we can become filled with the Holy Spirit.

Because when we pray and when we love, we are open to the Spirit of God, who is love.

These are the more obvious ways to breathe in the breath of God, but we all know that day-to-day family life involves a whole lot more than prayer and Scripture reading. But that doesn't mean we need to receive less of the Holy Spirit. God is *always* part of the present situation.

I once grew close to a wonderful Franciscan friar. True to his calling, he was a "joyful penitent." What was the source of his continuous joy? When I asked him, he told me, "The grace of the present moment." Over the years of family living, I have come to understand that phrase more and more. There truly is grace for each present moment.

There is always an opportunity to see the Lord's hand in our daily lives. As parents especially, it is important for us to seize the natural events that occur within the family and soak the Spirit out of the event. We should introduce our children to the Lord of the commonplace, the One who brings His mystery into what we perceive as the mundane.

Through all of the rites of passage, our children experience the pain of rejection, loneliness, insecurity, and a whole host of other emotions. As parents, we occupy positions of ministry, pastoring and caring for our families. In that sense, as well (1 Cor. 4:2; Luke 19:13), we have become stewards of the mysteries of God. Even though life in God's Holy Spirit involves incredible mystery, and even though we may not fully understand the mystery ourselves, we need to do our best to help our children receive the mysteries and workings of the Holy Spirit in their own lives.

Jesus did this for His disciples. He taught them as much as He could and then told them to wait for the Spirit. He would lead them in the way of truth (John 14:17). He said, "You will receive power when the holy Spirit comes upon you, and you will be my witnesses in Jerusalem, throughout Judea and Samaria, and to the ends of the earth" (Acts 1:8).

They waited. They waited for that power. They persevered, holding on to the promise of the Master. In fact, they actively sought after the promise not only in the upper room, but for the rest of their lives. Every day they asked God to fill them with the Spirit, and God was faithful to them. He will be to us.

This power confirmed their mission to live as Jesus did, proclaim His message and carry on His mission. He had told them that they would do greater things than He had done (John 14:12). In their humanness, they probably had some doubts, but things began to happen! Things happened because, by the Spirit, they had the Master's life within them. By the Spirit, they had power to do what Jesus did, power to be the Church, power to live the gospel, and that same power of the Holy Spirit is also available to us who live in the domestic church today.

I realize that many do not think that "pentecostal power" in the true sense of the word is available for us today, that it was necessary for the apostles, but not realistic for us. Still others fully believe in the power of the Spirit today but feel they are unworthy of the gift or perhaps simply do not know how to receive it. Frankly many people feel that it's too late to do anything to salvage their family. As Christians, we should remember the first rule of thumb: Nothing is impossible with God (Luke 1:37 NIV).

I know many couples who once saw their marriages as hopeless causes. Paul and Theresa are only one example. They were both raised in strong ethnic, Catholic homes. They fell in love, married at a young age, and began to raise a family. Like most newlyweds, they appeared fairly happy, but when the excitement of a new family wore thin, and the pressures of daily life increased, the marriage began to suffer. For some time, Paul and Theresa painfully considered divorce, but like so many other Christian families, they refused to give in to this escape hatch in obedience to their Church's teaching. They found a way out of this dilemma through discovering the power of the Spirit for their marriage and family.

Paul discovered that he was a son of God and that he could know God as a Father. Instead of simply reciting prayers, he began to pray deeply and personally. Theresa also discovered that, in spite of all the inadequacies she thought she had, she was precious in the sight of God. Her lifelong insecurity about her femininity, womanhood, and ability to be a wife and mother began to dissipate. Paul and Theresa experienced individual healing and then together as a couple. They began to see their role as parents, to co-pastor a "church in the home," their domestic church.

What had seemed hopeless began to change. They had power for family life. Some fifteen years later, Paul and Theresa stand together as an example of a holy and happy couple with a strong family structure. They still face problems, but they know a new source of power. Their children are not all perfect; they too have had their share of problems. Paul and Theresa's marriage is renewed, but it has not been all joy. They have struggled as any couple struggles, but they have found meaning and purpose even in the most difficult circumstances because they know they are not alone. They have a life with purpose as part of the family of God. And they have hope because of the power of the Holy Spirit. the Lord entered into Paul and Theresa's lives and into their home on a rescue mission. And for fifteen years, God has been at work, reassembling and rebuilding their family life. Paul and Theresa are one example of the many families in which God has manifested His power. My family is another example.

One could read this book and believe that my family is a more explicitly Christian version of Ozzie and Harriet. This is far from the truth. That 1950s image of family life, though entertaining, is often far from most peoples' daily reality and certainly far from ours. Our family life is full of mistakes. For example, mornings are often characterized by grumpiness (especially Dad's) rather than the pristine, energetic joy presented in those wonderful programs.

Maybe some of you have five children (or more). If so, you know what a challenge it is to love them all in the manner they deserve. I make a lot of mistakes and so does my wife. For that matter, so do the kids. But the Lord does not ask for perfection, only true affection—for one another, for Him. With five children,

He is constantly at work transforming us. His power is at work in every family that identifies itself with Jesus Christ, the Head of the Church, and the domestic church.

Unity

But power is not the only fruit of the Holy Spirit; He also brings unity. How much we need true unity in family life! Again, we look to the example of the early church. We have already seen how they were empowered to preach the gospel with boldness, and now we examine how they became one body, united under one Master. At first, they were a crowd of frightened followers huddled with the Mother of the Lord in the upper room, and then they became one unified Church that would indeed span the earth.

The Scriptures tell us, "All who believed were together and had all things in common" (Acts 2:44). They gave up their possessions, and they prayed. They loved the Lord and witnessed with joy and fervor. Signs and wonders were accomplished in their midst. They became a unified Church by the power of the Holy Spirit (Acts 2). So can our families. But we need to look to the Holy Spirit to accomplish this task as did the early believers.

It did not take long for the experience of unity in the Pentecost event to meet the challenge of disagreement. The Greek Jews complained against the Hebrew Jews because they weren't getting enough food (see Acts 6:1-7). Sounds like last night's dinner table discussion, doesn't it? They argued over whether Gentile Christians had to comply with the whole Mosaic Law (Acts 15). Again, sounds like the older children's demands on the younger ones. But in the midst of these very real disagreements, as well as the intense persecution, they encountered as they sought to make the gospel known, they found unity. How? Through the actions of the Holy Spirit. So can we in our daily domestic church life.

The early believers became one by learning to love one another with divine love, an agape love, a self-giving love, the same kind of love that propelled the Lord Himself to the cross. They discovered experientially what theologians have attempted to tell us through the ages. The Holy Spirit, Himself, is the source of divine love. The Holy Spirit is the love flowing between the Father and the Son, the love at work within the Godhead. As profound and incomprehensible as that may seem, that love is available to our families and can be the source of our love for one another. It was said of the early church by outsiders, "See how those Christians love one another!" May it be said of our families!

We must remember that love can only come from God; we can only love because He first loved us (1 John 4:10). Agape love cannot be summoned up by mere human effort. It requires a spark of the divine to change us, to make us Christ-like. But even though love is initiated by God, we have a responsibility to embrace and activate that love in our lives.

To love—how do we make concrete such an abstract concept? Jesus reveals to us ways of living out love. One of His greatest tangible acts of love occurred at the last supper where Jesus showed His love through serving. He got up from the table, took a basin, a towel, and washcloth and proceeded to move around the table washing the feet of the disciples (John 13:4–5). The God of the whole universe, who dwells in inaccessible light, in the flesh, was washing the feet of His followers. As the hands of divinity touched their feet. He said, "I have given you an example, and so you must do for one another."

Our Lord's action takes on even greater significance when we examine all of the symbolism. For instance, Jesus could have washed the head or hands of the disciples, but He chose to cleanse their feet. Feet are the lowest, dirtiest, and often the least attractive part of the human body, and the ones that receive the most wear and tear. Precisely in our dirt, in our sin, in our weariness does Jesus meet us to provide forgiveness, healing, and refreshment (Matt. 11:28).

Also profound about this scene is that Jesus, on possibly the most frightening and difficult night of His life, continued to teach and to serve. It would have been much easier to simply stay at the table and enjoy the companionship of His friends for the last time on earth. But Jesus got up. And He says to us by example, "Get up and out of your comfort zone, and love My family." He wants us to be patient and firm with the unruly, rebellious teenager, to stabilize the drug-addicted child, to be gentle and tender with the child in pain, to make peace with the angry spouse. Every day within the family, we have the opportunity to pick up the basin, towel, and washcloth and serve.

Do we serve one another in our families? Do we love one another unconditionally? Do we actively seek unity by following the example of Christ? Do we realize that Jesus is present with us by the power of the Holy Spirit? All too often we fall short, don't we? But the same Holy Spirit who was with the early church is with us. There is always a new beginning, another chance. After all, forgiveness is at the heart of the domestic church. The Holy Spirit permeates every aspect of our lives—in our homes, in our relationships with spouses and children, and in all our struggles. The Spirit is in the midst of the family because He is invested in our family life.

By the power of the Holy Spirit, we can become one in our home. We can learn and relearn how to love one another in sincerity and truth. We can learn to not only tolerate one another's weaknesses, but to urge one another on to holiness. In a very real way we can sanctify each other by loving one another with God's love. God has built the need for love into the very fabric of every person, and He continually calls all of us to activate that love, particularly within the confines of the domestic sanctuary.

Bring Forth the Kingdom of God

To the extent that we obey the urgings of the Spirit, to that extent will God use us and our families to bring about His kingdom. Jesus clearly indicates the need for the Holy Spirit as the agent for the kingdom. When Jesus walked with his disciples, they regularly asked him, "Lord, are you at this time going to restore the kingdom to Israel?" (Acts 1:6). On the final occasion of their asking, His answer was very interesting. He said, "You will receive power when the holy Spirit comes upon you" (Acts 1:8). At first glance, this does not seem to answer the question.

But Jesus did answer the question; he said to them and to us, "I have already done so. And I continue My mission through you. Through the power of my Holy Spirit, you will spread the kingdom. You will spread the reign of God. By your lives and your words, you will continue on in My task." God will build His kingdom through us. A prayer attributed to St. Teresa of Avila illustrates how the Lord wants to build the kingdom through us. Paraphrased, the words reveal a profound truth about the Incarnation: Christ has no body now; we are his earthly hands and feet now. Ours are the human eyes through which he looks with compassion on the people of this world. He has no feet with which to walk to do good, but ours. Through our hands he blesses the world. Christ has no body now on earth, but ours.

These moving words concretely portray what it means to be part of God's work, part of building the kingdom. In the New American Bible, the word that is translated as "kingdom" is also translated as "reign" or "rule." This concept of reign or rule is a helpful way for us as families to understand the work of the Holy Spirit in our homes. The Holy Spirit is at work in our families bringing about and expanding the reign of God, breaking into every aspect of our lives—our relationships, our recreation, our labor, our planning, our vacations, our finances, our decision making.

God is not interested simply in what we think of as "the spiritual." He is interested in the whole of life. He is interested in the way we love one another and live with one another, in the way we approach our daily activity, and in the way we view the world. Everything is to come under the dynamic reign of God.

In a recent letter addressed specifically to lay people, John Paul II said:

There cannot be two parallel lives in existence: on the one hand, the so-called "spiritual" life, with its values and demands; and on the other, the so-called "secular" life, that is, life in a family, at work, in social relationships, in the responsibilities of public life and in culture. . . . This split between the faith which many profess and their daily lives deserves to be counted among the more serious errors of our age.[1]

Practical Daily Living in the Spirit

Living by the power of the Holy Spirit under the reign and rulership of God isn't really all that complicated. It can and does happen in the Christian family. For example, for children this means living under godly parental authority. Parents stand in the shoes of God (and what big shoes to fill), so when children obey their parents, they obey those whom God has chosen to guide them. As adults, we need to learn how to submit to our spouse out of obedience to Christ. Paul tells us to "be subordinate to one another out of reverence for Christ"(Eph. 5:21). Spouses should serve one another in love and participate in the grace of "emptying out," following the Lord's example: "Who, though he was in the form of God, did not regard equality with God something to be grasped. Rather, he emptied himself, taking the form of a slave, coming in human likeness" (Phil. 2:6–7).

At all times, we should be able to ask ourselves, "Would God be pleased with the way I am loving my wife or my husband?" "Does the way I treat my children reflect my belief that they belong to Christ, and that He lives in them?" Of course, we cannot answer these questions with an affirmative response all the time, can we? Spiritual growth is a lifelong dynamic; God continues to work on us, and we continue to change. As Paul asserts, "Work out your salvation with fear and trembling" (Phil. 2:12ff).

The conversion process for those of us called to the married state and family life is worked out in the circumstances of our daily lives. We can become a domestic church where the kingdom of God, the reign of God, is demonstrated all the time. The key is perseverance and participation with the Lord in His plan.

Spiritual Gifts

We have so far explored the work of the Holy Spirit as He empowers us and promotes unity. But St. Paul talks of the Holy Spirit in another way that I think is significant for family life. From 1 Corinthians 2:11–12, we read:

Who knows what pertains to a person except the spirit of the person that is within? Similarly, no one knows what pertains to God except the Spirit of God. We have not received the spirit of the world but the Spirit that is from God, so that we may understand the things freely given us by God. (1 Cor. 2:11–12)

St. Paul speaks in this passage about the "spirit of the world." When the Bible talks about the world in this sense, it does not refer to trees and rivers and lakes and the created order, but rather to a system that has pushed God out and has put self in the center of all life. In this sense, we are surrounded by the "spirit of the world" and are often more deeply imbued with it than with the Spirit of our God. This is obviously not the Lord's plan; He wants us to be temples of His Holy Spirit. He wants to teach us His ways so that we can instruct our children in them. And what does He use as the instrument of instruction? That's right, the Holy Spirit!

The Spirit instructs us continually. The prophet Isaiah speaks of the sevenfold gifts of the Holy Spirit (Isa. 11:2–3) that all Christians receive at baptism—wisdom, understanding, knowledge, counsel, piety, fortitude, and fear of the Lord. As we allow these gifts to operate in our personal lives, our families can be transformed as well.

One of the main operations of the Spirit in our lives is to lead us into all truth, and He does this often by convicting us of our own sin. Thank the Lord that He shows us our sin so that we can repent and be free.

In the family, repentance can be taught and caught. We should teach our children about sin so that the Holy Spirit can convict them of it, and they in turn can acknowledge and turn from their sin. Structured family prayer times can be an opportunity to repent of sin verbally. Without shame, we have encouraged our children, at times in prayer, to acknowledge their sin before God and repent of it. We also try to lead by example in acknowledging and seeking forgiveness for our own sin. Certainly discretion must be used here, but I believe it sets a wonderful example when children learn that Mom and Dad need God's help and forgiveness too. They learn that we are teaching, correcting, leading, and serving not because we are perfect, but precisely because our position of leadership has been vested in us by the Lord. They will see that in a very special way through our seeking God's forgiveness openly, and when necessary, their forgiveness as well.

Also, confession truly is good for the soul. We will see a reservoir of freedom in our children's relationships with us and with their peers when they learn to "own up" to their actions, learn to repent, and receive the glorious freedom that is Christ's free gift.

I remember one example of this. My Annie was six years old. One evening in family prayer she asked the Lord's forgiveness for being selfish that day and not sharing with her younger sister. I had already heard about the incident from my wife, but watching the Holy Spirit work in her, leading her to truth and freedom, was beautiful. As Catholic Christians, for those who are old enough, we also encourage frequent sacramental confession in our family. It is a tremendous gift.

I realize that we live in an age that downplays sin, an age that all too often no longer calls sin, sin. But as a result of this alleged enlightenment, we seem to have raised a generation of children who are riddled with guilt. Contrary to what many modern thinkers say, justifying and blurring over sin does not free our children, but rather puts them into bondage. Repentance frees people from guilt—admitting our sin, acknowledging it, and asking forgiveness. When we shatter the obstacle of sin, then can we live in the truth of the Lord, and that truth will produce its fruit within the domestic church and the universal Church. Of course, there is the dilemma of false guilt and scrupulosity. That is another whole subject. But the difference between the two is usually discernible by the fruit. The Holy Spirit convicts us of sin to lead us to freedom, not ongoing guilt and condemnation.

We have taken a rather extensive look at the workings of the Holy Spirit, but there is so much more that can be said. From our exploration, it is clear that we need the power of the Holy Spirit to mold our families so that we can become what God has called us to be, the domestic church, the Church in miniature, a sign of God's glory to the world.

This is not a vision that can be fully attained by families without Christ. Without Him, families are assemblies of people with a wonderful natural bond. But only with Christ can a family become a domestic church. Why settle for less, now that you know the full provision?

4

The Domestic Cross

My father had a heart attack last year. More than 40 percent of his heart no longer functions. The news hit me like a brick. My father and mother lived in Florida (still do), quite a distance from Steubenville, Ohio, where I lived at the time, and so family visits had been fewer than we'd have liked. Thank God I was able to spend a significant amount of time with my dad during his recovery. The visit with him was not simply a service from a dutiful son; it was also an occasion to reaffirm my love for him. And I had the chance to give him the first copy of my book *Evangelical Catholics*. I vividly remember inscribing within the cover, "The first book to the first man who revealed the love of God the Father to me." I knew at that moment the Lord was using that opportunity as a means of healing between my father and me.

I was filled with great love for my father. A love that was born of struggle, but as a result, is strong and well rooted. It has taken me years to learn the fundamental truth that his vital role in my life was not earned by his perfection, but by his position. He was and is my earthly father. Position, not perfection. So it is with my role and yours in the lives of our children. We have been strategically placed by God in their lives. So it is with my own dad.

Well, we had a long series of discussions together while he was in the hospital. Suffering brings out a depth in people that is often lost in the hustle and bustle of daily living. Times of suffering seem to bring the family together, regardless of past hurts or issues that have gone unforgiven or undiscussed.

It was a difficult time with my father, difficult to face some of the issues that we talked about and very difficult to watch him suffer. But as I increasingly come to understand, difficulty and blessing often go hand in hand in family life.

On a very different level, the struggles occur on my own home front as well. My teenage daughter misunderstood me again last month. We seem to have this problem a lot.

We recently moved to Virginia, and Kristen began attending a public high school in our city. After about a month, she brought home a blue piece of paper and asked me to sign it. She indicated that the teacher had forgotten to get parental permission before beginning the "Family Life Education" class. The paper only cursorily explained what the class involved, but we quickly realized that it was a sex education class.

Kristen and her mom had long since discussed the gift of her sexuality. The two have a very open, healthy relationship, and Kristen feels free to talk over her questions and issues with Laurine. But upon investigation of the class curriculum, we became very concerned. We did not agree with the perspective being taught in the class. We also felt offended by the school's attitude toward parental involvement and its lack of openness about the subject matter. We told Kristen she needed to withdraw from the class. Because the class had already begun (without parental consent), she thought the whole experience would be too embarrassing. But we insisted, and as is too often the case, I did so forcefully and insensitively. Kristen was hurt, but she obeyed our instructions.

I realize that I have difficulty communicating at times, and the father/teenage-daughter age barrier accentuates the problem. In this instance, as good as my intentions were, Kristen again experienced my directions as one more debilitating experience of correction. Although I still believe I needed to redirect her that time, I do try to respect her privacy and increasing maturity. It's tough, this communication challenge, especially with teenagers. (And

I'm certain that Kristen thinks communication is especially difficult with dads!)

However, time heals wounds, and we have grown much in this
month. Our decision has proven to be the best one and has also
given us a good opportunity to work with the school officials. I
imagine that our growth will continue as the months go on. There
are so many experiences like this in the daily stuff of family life. I
could list so many other examples from our family. But I am certain that you have your own domestic landscape cluttered with
struggles and pain, disappointments and wounds, and the real
nitty-gritty stuff of working out Christian family living in the
trenches of this world.

Don't Forget the Cross

In the previous chapter, we took joy in examining the gifts of
the Holy Spirit, the power given to us from on high. As we have
already said, this is the power we all need to live out our call as
domestic churches. I hope you have rejoiced in your own personal
Pentecost and perhaps see even more clearly the mini-
pentecosts that often sustain Christian family living.

Though Pentecost is a wonderful gift to the universal Church,
the domestic church, and individual Christians, church history
reveals that shortly after Pentecost, the early church was put to
the test. They experienced the reign not only of power, but also
of persecution and pain, often leading to violent death. The power
of the Holy Spirit seemed to manifest itself in a different way
during this time. He became the Church's source of strength.
At that time, God's power was absolutely necessary for perseverance, courage, and hope in the midst of these very real
struggles.

The Holy Spirit bolstered the early disciples' courage and empowered them to *become* church, even in the midst of fear. They
were called to preach the good news to every nation "in season
and out of season." Although at times it seemed that the seed of
the good news fell on deaf ears, God's grace continued to enable

the disciples to fulfill their call. His grace met them in the heart of every struggle, every doubt, every fear, and every cross.

So it is with us. There will be crosses for our families. There will be pain and struggle. There will be misunderstandings, hurt, fear, and doubt. There will be crosses in the domestic church. The lives of the apostles and the history of the church (which is our universal family that has preceded us in the faith) demonstrate that we can never have Pentecost without seeing the silhouette of the cross in the distance. We can't have the power without having the pain. Power and pain consistently seem to embrace in the stuff of daily Christian family living.

A Christian mind cannot dwell on Pentecost and ignore the cross. The cross is a necessary element of our life, and it has marvelous power all its own. The cross and the Pentecost experience complement rather than oppose each other. The cross of Christ preceded Pentecost, and the crosses of His disciples followed Pentecost. The cross before us, the cross behind us, the cross with us. And God helps us lift them onto our shoulders and walk.

As baptized Christians we experienced the crucifixion of the old man or woman, the resurrection of the new, and the release of God's Spirit within us to abide in that new life. Pentecost and the cross, the two are meant to be constantly intertwined throughout our lives. Pentecost will always be a very real part of our lives, but so will the cross. We cannot avoid either. They are our salvation and our glory.

Lord, You Picked the Wrong Cross

I remember a story I heard in the early days of my faith walk that has stuck with me through the years. I did not understand it then and still don't fully, I'm sure. But something about this tale always strikes a chord somewhere deep in my heart.

There once was a faithful Christian man who lived his life in simplicity, always ready to serve the Lord. But the man had a heavy cross attached to his back, an awkward cross that always seemed to be in his way. Every morning when the man awoke, he struggled to break the cross from his back. He tried everything to get rid of it, thinking, *If only I could be freed of this burden, I could serve God better.* It's not that he didn't want a cross, but this particular cross just didn't coincide with his vision of suffering.

One day he heard about a factory that housed crosses of all shapes and sizes. The idea intrigued him. As he investigated this factory, he discovered that he could actually trade in his cross for one that fit him a little better. Overjoyed, he rushed to the warehouse where he told the gatekeeper his whole saga. Moved with pity, the gatekeeper stretched out his hand and mysteriously lifted the burden from his back and sent the man on his search.

Unexpectedly, the search took hours and hours. There were so many crosses to choose from, but they were either too big, too small, too heavy, or too light. Some looked very attractive, but the man knew somehow they weren't for him. Finally, after a long and arduous search, there it was—the perfect cross for him. His heart was bursting at how his life would change. He would be able to handle this cross. It was just right.

With a new hope and great joy, the man left the warehouse and approached the gatekeeper saying, "I have finally found the cross for me!" The gatekeeper replied, "Oh, it's you—the perfect fit. And coincidentally, it is the exact same cross with which you came here. I put it back in stock."

Obviously the man learned a great lesson in humility, but he also learned (and we can learn along with him) that God's knowledge of our lives is complete, and that every trial He allows fits us for some reason. God promised as well that He would never tempt us beyond our strength (1 Cor. 10). We cannot exchange God's call on our life and remain fully alive. It is rather only when we embrace the call that we will most fully come to life. Part of the call is the cross. Every cross that we carry can lead us more deeply into the heart of God's plan for our lives.

Living in the Christian family affords us daily opportunities to shoulder our crosses. In fact, I believe day-to-day living is the cross of family life. If we begin to see the cross as a means to glory, then we can begin to see the domestic cross as a means to glory for the domestic church. In other words, the long-term purpose of the vocation of marriage (like any vocation) is as a means to our salvation and our glory. That long-term goal is met through the short-term daily experience of sanctification in the home. The daily crosses taken up in the home are actually sanctifying when seen as part of God's call on our lives.

Change of Perspective

The modern mind is accustomed to avoiding pain and suffering in any way. We have every kind of extra-strength pain reliever. We have drugs of all types. We have liquid that numbs the pain. We turn to alcohol and drugs and often sex in order to cover over pain. We don't like pain. So for many, this message of the domestic cross will be as typically unwelcomed as any other pain in our lives.

In order to be able to embrace this realistic but unappealing theology, what we really need is a renewal of the mind, *a change of perspective that enables us to see the value of suffering.*

We need a renewed context in which to view Christian family life. For some, the only way to gain this new perspective will be to retrain our fundamental thinking: to see the value of ordinary crosses within family life as having been sanctified by Christ with the intention of making us like Him. There are countless events in the home that allow us to take on this perspective. Literally hundreds of times daily. How many times do we stop and ask ourselves throughout the day, "Why am I doing this?" (substitute for "this" any of the following: going to work, paying bills I didn't know I had, listening to my children tell me how little I understand them, etc.).

We need to train ourselves in the midst of these difficulties to remember the eternal perspective. If we can make a habit of remembering that we do all things for God and from Him we will ultimately receive blessing, our response can eventually change. This transformation all begins, finds its continuation, and ends with a renewed mind, as Paul says in his letter to the Roman Christians (Rom. 12:2).

I have personally had to embrace, and I mean *embrace,* this renewal of mind in my own home. Laurine and I have been blessed with five wonderful children. They are good kids at heart, but they are still kids. Each one of them has presented us with our share of joys and victories, as well as sorrows and pain. Our life together as a family has certainly not been easy. In the midst of our sorrow and pain, quite truthfully it has been difficult to welcome the struggle as the road to our sanctification. But as we all know, Jesus never promised that the Christian life would be easy. In fact, He exhorts the disciples anew in every generation, "Unless a man deny himself and pick up his cross daily, he will have no part of me" (Matt. 16:24; Luke 9:23).

A particularly trying time for my family was my first year of law school. Many of you who have experienced the first year of law school (or perhaps heard about it) know that it far exceeds the worst nightmare of fraternity hazing. But unlike hazing, it seems to never end. It goes on and on and never stops. There were so many times when I was on the verge of collapse, but somehow we all just kept going. The comfort of the undergraduate years where professors stood at the front of the class and instructed was ripped out from underneath me. Now they asked questions, seemingly endless questions, day after day until my mind began to overload. To increase the pressure, there was only a single examination for the entire semester's work, and the whole grade rested upon it. I recall how nervous and frightened I was. *Finals Week!* Even now, I get a knot in my stomach as I remember it!

As if the trials of law school weren't enough, I also was very aware of the daily challenge of a new marriage. Laurine and I were only in our second year of marriage, still somewhat newlyweds, and we had a beautiful baby girl named Kristen Renee (the name means "reborn Christian").

I certainly was not the only one who struggled that year. Laurine had her own share of difficulties. She had to go back to work because of my law school bills and the general cost of living, and so together with her work and the odd jobs I was able to do at school, we barely made ends meet.

Laurine and I did all that we could to provide a safe and comfortable home for our daughter. But not even Kristen could escape the struggle of the domestic cross. She was as open as any of us to the sanctifying power of trial and the struggles of life. But Kristen was so helpless it broke my heart. I remember she was very, very sick and rarely slept. She cried incessantly, couldn't keep her food down, had terrible bowel movements, and was consistently ill.

I vividly remember the day I was called out of class to attend to Kristen in her sickness. I immediately took her to the doctor's office and found that day there was a substitute doctor. He examined my little girl, and after what seemed like an endless amount of time, he came out of the room in a stupor, his face painted a solemn gray. "Mr. Fournier, could we discuss your daughter?" he asked. Immediately fear gripped me. My greatest fears were fulfilled as he proceeded to tell me he thought Kristen had cystic fibrosis.

To somewhat numb ears, he attempted to explain the etymology of this disease and what might be the outcome. All I heard was what might be the outcome—continual degeneration of the muscles and possible death. But he wanted to take her through further tests. At that point, there was hardly a hope in my heart. I held my baby in my arms. It took all the strength I had to even hold her close to my heart. I literally felt my entire world collapsing inside. I took Kristen to the car, and as soon as we got in, I cried out, "My God, my God, please come to our aid!"

By the time I arrived home to our tiny apartment, Laurine was home from work. I opened the door, and she knew there was something terribly wrong. I put Kristen down in her crib and with tears rolling down my cheek proceeded to tell my wife the news. We held one another and wept and together fell to our knees and cried. We may have been there for hours.

Any parent reading this is most likely knows the fear of losing a child. That is pain. And that is the cross.

We struggled for weeks, turning to God and begging His mercy, trying to believe that there was a plan in all of this for us. We faltered and doubted many times, but there was really nowhere else to go but to God. As it turned out, when our regular doctor returned, he told us that the analysis was incorrect. Further tests confirmed his thoughts. Kristen merely had serious allergies that would eventually work themselves out.

God answered our prayer for mercy, and as the years have gone by, we realize that part of God's plan was to build our faith. And it did. The experience changed our relationship with God and brought to it a new dimension of trust. Moreover, our love for one another deepened and grew. These are the kinds of fruits that we can experience only through the pain of the cross.

Kristen's illness wasn't the only cross. Over the years, Keith, Ann, MaryEllen, and now Joel have followed suit. But we continue to build on that perspective of renewal and try to see inconveniences, illnesses, rebellion, misunderstandings, as well as joys, victories, celebrations, and good-morning hugs as all part of the same package wrapped up in the love and concern of God, our Father.

One More Hurdle

Our humanness forbids us to respond perfectly in every situation and so, like everything in the Christian life, renewal of the mind requires a continual change, a continually fresh perspective, a constant change in our thinking. Laurine and I have gone through many stages as we try to work our way through struggle. We thought we hit the worst with Kristen's illness, but as more children came and the pressures increased, it didn't get easier like we thought it would.

We kept thinking that things would always get easier, a perspective that we now call "the hurdle mentality." Maybe you live like that too. Every time we went through a new pain, we would say, "As soon as we get over this hump, things will be normal." We were married in my last year of college, and at one point I was taking 21 credit hours and working 40 hours a week. Laurine, meanwhile, was immediately gifted with a child. Needless to say, the pressure was on from the moment our marriage began. We thought, "as soon as I get out of school, things will be normal." Then law school followed. So too the gift of more children, more pressures, and more responsibility.

For years we persisted in the hurdle mentality. We said, "Well, when law school is finished," or "When I pass the bar," or "When I'm through with this pregnancy," or "When I lose all of this excess weight," or "When we're through with this illness," or "When I find a better job," or "When these bills are finally paid," or "When we close on our first house." The list could go on indefinitely.

We all have a list, don't we? Laurine and I have come to see that struggle, pressure, hard work, mistakes, confusion, pain, hurt . . . these are normal. They are an ordinary part of human existence. *No,* life is not all about pain and struggle, but certainly it weaves its way into all areas of life. What makes that bearable is a twofold gift: Along with the struggle comes the rich joy of knowing God's loving hand in the midst of our trial; along with struggle comes celebration, play, and victory. They are all part of life in God's family.

I know it is difficult, and I know that many will instinctively reject this way of thinking. But in truth, struggle will not go away, so to deal with it peaceably and effectively, this renewed perspective needs to be captured, cultivated, and continued daily. Then will our families be able to survive and cooperate with God's grace and become the domestic church He intends us to be.

Renewal of the Mind

Paul in Romans 12 explains the principle with which each one of us and our families can be transformed:

Offer your bodies as a living sacrifice, holy and pleasing to God, your spiritual worship. Do not conform yourself to this age but be transformed by the renewal of your mind, that you may discern what is the will of God, what is good and pleasing and perfect. (Rom. 12:1-2)

Paul is saying the same thing to the Christian church. We need a new way of thinking. Our contemporary culture teaches that self-gratification, self-fulfillment, and self-enhancement are the ultimate goals. Or an equally false yet more subtle deception is that all our families need is better communication, more honesty, and cooperation. Certainly these are all necessary for growth and maturity within our familial relationships; however, caring for the psychological and emotional dimension is not enough without God.

We cannot conform to this worldly approach to marriage and family life. Rather, we should allow God to transform and raise our marriage to the level of church living. The vocation of marriage and family is about more than healthy emotional relationships. Marriage in its full and sacred truth is about love. Loving means laying down our own life, sacrificing ourselves. Jesus told us that there is no greater love than this (John 15:13).

Isn't this what Paul is also saying? "Offer your bodies as living sacrifices." In other words, we are to place our whole selves, everything that makes us alive—our heart, mind, emotions, and will—at the service of God. If God has called us to serve as husbands, wives, parents, or children, we are to offer everything we have in that service. This is the mindset we should have toward our marriages. Our homes are "to be transformed" as we begin to see our families less as a responsibility and more as the instrument God is using to work out our salvation.

Living Sacrifices

Once one sees the value of the cross within the family or at least sees the purpose of it, it follows that the next step is action. Changing our thinking is painful, but acting it out is even more difficult. Sacrificing daily is the difficult part. Many times during the day we are called to die to our own desires. Whether they be to sleep, to be alone, to get out of the house, to not have to cook, to leave the dishes in the sink and the clothes on the floor. Instead we sacrifice for the good of the family, and it is in these very sacrifices that we are going to be transformed.

This notion of sacrifice is critical. God has given us in the family people through whom we can grow holy, people that as we sacrifice for them will lead us to holiness. In a certain sense, our families become the friends that John writes about in his Gospel when he speaks of laying down life for friends (John 15:13). Or what the writer of Matthew means when he quotes Jesus saying that the second greatest commandment is to love our neighbor (Matt. 22:39). Sometimes we forget that our families are part of the neighborhood. They are our closest neighbors. C. S. Lewis, in his masterpiece *The Weight of Glory,* speaks to this notion of the holiness and the glory of our neighbors.

> Meanwhile, the cross comes before the crown and tomorrow is a Monday morning. . . . It may be possible for each to think too much of his own potential glory hereafter; it is hardly possible for him to think too often or too deeply about that of his neighbor. The load, or weight, or burden of my neighbor's glory should be laid daily on my back. . . . It is a serious thing to live in a society of possible gods and goddesses, to remember that the dullest and most uninteresting person you talk to may one day be a creature which, if you saw it now, you would be strongly tempted to worship. . . . All day long we are, in some degree, in the light of these overwhelming possibilities, it is with the awe and the circumspection proper to them, that we should conduct all our dealings with one another, all friendships, all loves, all play, all politics.[1]

Substitute for *neighbor, mother* or *father* or *brother* or *sister.* Don't just limit the use of *neighbor* to the couple down the street. We ought to reverence all human beings as our neighbors, and that applies especially to those with whom we live. So when we die to ourselves and live for our neighbor in the family, that is an incarnate expression of love.

Waking up every hour with your five-month-old child, endlessly cooking and cleaning for the family, understanding the rebellious teenager, persevering together when escape is the easier answer, loving one another when you don't feel the emotion any more. These are difficult moments, but all of these thorns of family life actually become the transforming vehicles that make us more like Jesus and prepare us to reign with Him.

Extending our love unconditionally in these situations builds our patience, tolerance, love, service, and selflessness. These are opportunities for us to be lifted up by God's strength when we no longer have any and to move in His power. That is when we can become the most effective servants of God. As we persevere through these trials, we begin to recognize and affirm our own faithfulness to God's call on our life. The fruit of that recognition is peace. Suddenly we begin to realize that all of these difficult moments are part of the plan. Then and only then can we allow them to lead us to the goal—holiness.

The word *holiness* means to be set apart for God's use or in other words, completely surrendered to His plan. Holiness is simply being faithful to that plan.

Again, Lewis speaks to the reality of the holiness of our families and friends. They, too, are set aside for God's purpose and, therefore, should be treated with incredible respect, dignity, and love.

> Our charity must be a real and costly love, with deep feeling for the sins in spite of which we love the sinner. . . . Next to the Blessed Sacrament itself, your neighbor is the holiest object presented to your senses. If he is your Christian neighbor he is holy in almost the same way, for in him also Christ *vere latitat*—the glorifier and the glorified, Glory Himself, is truly hidden.[2]

In Faithfulness There Is Peace

The experience of daily faithfulness is what allows family life to sanctify all of those who respond to the call. But it is important to always remember that the domestic church, like the whole Church, while divinely ordained is still a human institution. The divine is continually manifested but only as it is intertwined with the human element. If we seek a perfect existence, a perfect marriage, a perfect church, a perfect family we will be discouraged, frustrated, angry, and always hurt. No family will ever be perfect. No church will ever be perfect. No existence will ever be perfect until the final resurrection. We need to accept our lack of perfection and work with it. We are a community of believers linked on the road to perfection, and perfection only reaches its completion in the glory of a face-to-face encounter with God. Only then will we be like Him for we will see Him as He is (1 John).

And it is grace that will lead us on the road to perfection. Only grace can somehow carve our difficult moments into the domestic cross. We need to rely on grace just as the early apostles did. And just as they were martyred in faithfulness to their call, so we as the domestic church must embrace the daily martyrdom of family life if we are to live in faithfulness to our call as church.

Sanctifying the Mundane

So often daily life in the family becomes frustratingly mundane. If you are like me, a doer and an action-oriented person, this may be a more obvious burden. At times, raising a family doesn't seem to be enough. Everybody raises a family. Some may feel, I know I have, they want to *do more* for God or serve the church in a tangible way. I am a man who has the gospel deeply rooted in his heart and have since a teenage conversion. I love to share the good news, and I take great joy in any opportunity that the Lord provides for me to do so. As a younger man, I pictured myself preaching to the nations and winning soul after soul to Christ.

Part of this desire was heartfelt, but much of it was simply disguised ego. Nonetheless it so preoccupied me that I too often evaluated my "work for the Lord" with a misguided romantic ideal of ministry. If it didn't match up with my notions of the way I thought the Lord wanted to work, I became discouraged and depressed. I wanted to do something extraordinary for God. I wanted to be an extraordinary servant for God.

Years later, a bit more seasoned and somewhat mellowed, I now see that the reality for me was not that I wanted to serve God in any way He wanted. Rather, I wanted the way that was different from most people. I wanted the superhero track. I thought I was being humble and sincerely wanted to steward the gifts that God had given me. Instead, I fell into a constant pattern of overdrive, incessant workaholism, and eventually a near-burnout situation.

But God has taught me much through that experience. I have learned that the extraordinary way is not my call. I am called to settle peacefully in the heart of my ordinary vocation, as husband, as father, as layman, and as lawyer. And to the extent that I more peacefully nestle into God's plan for my life, I experience great peace.

The Ordinary Vocation

It is necessary that we are clear about the use of the word *ordinary* as I am using it here. In my tradition as a Catholic Christian, marriage and family life has always been spoken of as the "ordinary vocation." The word *ordinary* is used not in any way to denigrate its value, but rather to demonstrate that the vocation of marriage and family is the norm. By far, the normal way men and women are sanctified and prepared for heaven is through the vehicle of Christian family life, the domestic church. That's right! Our families are our means to sanctification, our training school for ministry, and our preparation for heaven.

In my earlier years, I often struggled with the call to marriage and family as being a holy calling. At times I have thought that those living life single for the Lord or living celibate lives can tend to greater holiness. The truth is that many do. But a more profound truth is that we are all called to holiness of life no matter what our vocation. Our paths to sanctity are just different. The leaders of my church put it this way:

> This holiness of the Church is constantly shown forth in the fruits of grace which the Spirit produces in the faithful and so it must be; it is expressed in many ways by the individuals who, each in his own state of life, tend to the perfection of love, thus sanctifying others; . . . it is therefore quite clear that all Christians in any state or walk of life are called to the fullness of Christian life and the perfection of love.[3]

I realize that many believe holiness is a result of praying several hours a day, or choosing difficult goods in tempting situations, or serving on every church committee possible. Actually, it is not so much in the difficult moments but in the nitty-gritty day-to-day life that we will be tested. There is nothing glamorous or heroic about daily life in the home. In fact, in a recent popular film called *Parenthood,* Steve Martin comments on family life: "I hate family; it's messy." And it is. But that's part of the plan. In the midst of diapers and discipline, puberty and poverty, we find a treasure that will never fade and wisdom that endures forever.

Though family life may seem to be mundane on the surface, we can always look deeper and see the incredible depth and mystery to God's creation and all of our seemingly ordinary activity. To allow the mundane to make us holy, we need to believe that the mundane is holy. Tom Howard, in his book entitled *Hallowed Be This House,* describes how the ordinary daily life of the family is holy ground. He suggests that anyone who thinks about the ordinary routine of life

> knows that what lies about him in his ordinary routines does, in fact, speak of more than its immediate function. It opens out onto vistas that stretch beyond our seeing, into the realm of mystery. Human bodies, for instance, are somehow images of God; work has something to do with our role as lords of creation; eating is a physical case in point of the nourishment that our inner man

needs; sleep is a small metaphor of death; and so forth. Ordinariness, in a word, opens out onto mystery, and the thing that men are supposed to do with mystery is to hallow it, for it all belongs to the Holy One. . . . We do in fact, walk daily among the hallows; and that our task now is exactly what Abel's or Solomon's was; namely, to offer whatever we do have, in the presence of the divine mysteries, as a continual oblation. To do this, of course, we will have to recover the sense of the hallowed as being all around us. We will have to open our eyes and try to see once more the commonplace as both cloaking and revealing the holy to us. We will have to refuse resolutely the secularism that has made ordinariness unholy.[4]

Having begun this chapter with a story about my teenage daughter, it seems only fitting to conclude with a tribute to her. Last weekend she asked to go to a party at a friend's house. Though this was a new friend, we were assured that her parents were home and that the party was properly supervised.

As I drove her down a country road to her destination, we were almost run off the road by two carloads of teenage boys. "Kristen," I said, "if those cars are at this party, you're coming home!"

Well, when I pulled down the long driveway, there they were. *Now what?* I thought to myself. I was concerned for Kristen's feelings and didn't want to embarrass her. For better or worse, I let her out of the car and told her to call me for a ride home. I told her I loved her and trusted her, but because I cared so much I wasn't comfortable leaving her here. She told me not to worry, but I drove away apprehensively.

Less than thirty minutes later, Kristen called me. "Dad, you were right about this one. Please come get me!"

I ended up taking seven other teenagers home too. Apparently the parents of the host had stayed in the basement, seemingly unaware of a dangerous situation developing upstairs when uninvited guests crashed the party.

After we had dropped off her friends, Kristen repeated, "Dad, you were right. This party was bad. I didn't know many of the kids, and I shouldn't have gone. Thanks for coming to get me and taking all my friends home too."

I hugged her, proud of her courage and good judgment. It was an ordinary moment, but a holy one. God's hand is resting firmly on His daughter.

5

The Wounded and the Lame

We have laid out a vision for Christian family life and examined a source of power that can help the family turn their vision into reality. We have explored the joy and sorrow of marriage and family life. It's almost overwhelming, isn't it?

You may be thinking now that you wish your family could actually fit into the vision of the domestic church, but it is not really for you. Or you may feel that your family is not "holy enough" or perhaps "not committed enough" to each other to make it work. Maybe the problem is brokenness or dysfunctionality. Maybe sickness or death has put a strain on your family. Maybe there is continual wrongdoing and unconfessed sin or patterns of sin. Whatever the reason, we often see our families as too wounded for this healthy vision, so we fail to pursue it.

This despair is understandable when we see the alcoholic parent, the drug-addicted son, the sexually addicted daughter, the delinquent teenagers, the self-centered love that often divides husbands and wives, the lack of peace in so many homes, the lack of focus on God. We see our failure to be patient, loving, firm, and balanced toward our children. We see our children, who are often totally absorbed in their own problems and have no desire to enter into family functions.

Many see all of this and feel that it's too late, that their families are already past the point of repair. These families see themselves as incapable of renewal and far from being a model of Christian living for other families. But renewal and witness are precisely God's plan, and God never calls us to something without the accompanying grace to live that call.

Unfortunately, however, instead of responding fully to the grace, families can become consumed by the woundedness that this age has all too often caused. Even when positive steps are possible, we tend to live in the pain, trapped, with no motivation to fight.

But even if there are tremendous wounds (in fact, *especially* if there are wounds), our families fit into God's plan. Some may think, "I'm not worthy," "I don't have the time or energy," or "I'm unhealthy and my kids are out of control." Whatever the issue, we all fit into the picture. It is precisely our woundedness that allows us to grasp even more tightly the suffering of Christ.

Instead of seeing pain as an obstacle to growth in the Lord and a stumbling block to building up our families, we should see our wounds as the very things that qualify us for Christian family life. It is in our brokenness, in our helplessness, that we may finally embrace the domestic cross and allow God to build the spiritual edifice of our home.

In a beautiful book of the Old Testament, the Lord prophesied through Micah that He would assemble the lame and make of them a remnant: "On that day, says the LORD, I will gather the lame, and I will assemble the outcasts, and those whom I have afflicted. I will make of the lame a remnant, and of those driven far off a strong nation" (Micah 4:6–7). God did not say He would raise up the mighty and conquer with them. He said he would bind together the weak, the lame, the wounded, and set them apart for His purpose.

All of us limp in some way. All of us are called to be this remnant. God has called our generation of wounded families to heal a wounded world. Contemporary family life is more often characterized by division and struggle than unity and tranquility. So many issues seem to emanate from the broken shell of the contemporary family.

Joseph

But as broken as the contemporary family seems, there is nothing new about many of the issues. If we want to talk about a family that was dealing with issues, let's talk about an ancient family. The story of Joseph, Jacob's son, and his brothers is recalled in the book of Genesis, beginning with chapter 37. The Scriptures tell us that the brothers were jealous of Joseph because he was the favored son. (Sound familiar?) That jealousy festered into bitterness and anger, rooted so deeply that they even wanted to murder their brother. Instead, they sold him into slavery but told their father that Joseph had been killed.

Much happened to Joseph in his time away from his family, but God eventually blessed him because he was a faithful and honest servant. As the story goes, years later Joseph had the opportunity to avenge the sin of his brothers, but he chose instead to forgive. The entire family was reunited then through Joseph's generosity and love. The sons of Jacob, the brothers of Joseph, became the twelve tribes of Israel, the fathers of God's people. The Lord built nations from a family laden with sin and weakness, selfishness, greed, and hatred. He still does.

So when we begin to despair about how our children don't get along or how much sin is part of our family's life, remember the story of Joseph. It took one person, Joseph, to be faithful and righteous. God only needs one instrument through which to begin blessing our families.

And that instrument need not be perfect, just available, brutally honest, and open to God's transforming love. The Scriptures overflow with examples of men and women who have been available, honest, and open.

David

One such hero of the faith is David, the shepherd boy turned king, whose faith is held up for all of us as an example. It was from his own line that the Son of God would come. David has always been a great example to me. Paul the apostle preached about the history of God's dealings with His people. He refers to David in Acts 13:22, "After removing Saul, he made David their king. He testified concerning him, 'I have found David, son of Jesse, a *man after my own heart;* he will do everything I want him to do'" (emphasis added). What a tribute and what a lesson!

Too often we remember the highlights of David's life—his slaying of Goliath, his wonderful carefree praise of the Lord, his wisdom, judgment, and leadership. But do we remember the David who succumbed to the sin of the flesh, the David who sent Uriah the Hittite to the front line of battle so that he would be killed? And for what reason did he do this? Because David lusted after Bathsheba, Uriah's wife. In fact, he took her to himself and committed the sin of adultery. At least to me, and perhaps to many of you, it would seem at this point that God would be through with a man like that. But He wasn't. Our God is the God of the second chance. David was not only a man after God's own heart in the midst of victory, but a man after God's own heart in the midst of defeat, sin, and pain. He was brutally honest and open to God's transforming love, a love that is often manifested through judgment and correction.

In 2 Samuel 12, the Lord, in His love, sends the prophet Nathan to David. Nathan spoke in allegorical language about a poor man and a little ewe lamb. The poor man was Uriah; the ewe lamb, his wife. He spoke as well about a rich man who, instead of taking his own sheep, took that one ewe lamb. He posed the question to David: How would the king deal with the case if it were brought before him? The Scripture tells us,

> David burned with anger against the man and said to Nathan, "As surely as the LORD lives, the man who did this deserves to die! He must pay for that lamb four times over, because he did such a thing and had no pity." Then Nathan said to David, *"You are the man!"* (2 Sam. 12:5–7 NIV, emphasis added)

David could have denied that prophetic correction from the

heart of God, but he didn't. As the prophet outlined David's transgression in detail, David was cut to the heart. The Scripture then describes David's forthright honesty: "Then David said to Nathan, 'I have sinned against the LORD'" (2 Sam. 12:13 NIV). One of the great characteristics of David's love for God was his quick repentance, his willingness to change and be corrected.

Dysfunctionality Doesn't Mean Death

I believe one of the reasons the Lord has preserved for us in the sacred Scripture the testimony of men like David and other men and women of faith who have made mistakes and persevered is so that we can be encouraged in our own personal lives. Perhaps we have not transgressed in the same way. But all of us (in the words of Paul to the Roman Christians) "have sinned and fall short of the glory of God" (Rom. 3:23 NIV). If perfection were the prerequisite to this path of holiness, none of us would qualify. There is but one perfect One, and His sacrificial love on the cross opened the door for the rest of us.

We all have been wounded and scarred by life. In this day and age, those wounds run deep. Many experts tell us that the overwhelming majority of Americans suffer from the fruit of dysfunctional families—families touched by divorce, addiction, abuse, separation, trauma, or tragedy. In these instances, the sins of the fathers are indeed visited upon the children: "I, the LORD your God, am a jealous God, punishing the children for the sin of the fathers to the third and fourth generation (Exod. 20:5 NIV).

The reality of dysfunctional family life is staggering. Twelve Step programs and other support groups have multiplied unbelievably in our day. These are positive and helpful resources. However, we cannot allow a label to lock us into a life without renewal and transformation. The goal of these groups is not dependency, but honest admission and recovery.

We need to see the truth of dysfunctionality. There are definite behavioral, emotional, and thought patterns that may be a result of a difficult life, or even the destructive effect of addiction.

I have received many wounds over the years that have left me with certain behavioral and emotional patterns that are not necessarily in God's order. These are a fruit of my own family life and the "law of sin and death." For so long, I failed to see my own weakness and chose instead to remain in denial. I had not learned to "boast of my weakness" as did St. Paul. I tried instead to live a "perfect" life. But for me it bore the rotten fruit of guilt, self-condemnation, and disillusionment.

The same may be true in your family. Maybe in your childhood, your parents always reinforced negative behavior. Perhaps codependency has always been at the heart of your personal relationships, even your family relationships, and you don't know any other way to love. Maybe there was no experience of affirmation or affective love, and you're still desperately in need of a hug. Maybe emotional, physical, or sexual abuse occurred. Maybe some of these things and others are true, but we do not have to be doomed to a minimal Christian life, a life of being less than God wants us to be. There is hope for the hopeless because of Jesus Christ.

The power of God can change things that human effort alone cannot. I am not promoting a disguised "health and wealth" gospel or a Christian life devoid of pain. I am suggesting that *in* and *through* our pain, God can perfect His power in our lives. Then we will be able to provide strength for others.

This whole issue of suffering, woundedness, and brokenness has plagued many because it is one of the most difficult paradoxes in the Christian life. All too often we blame God for our suffering and, therefore, fail to plumb its deep meaning. We try to rid ourselves of the pain by ignoring or denying it. The truth, though, is that all of us have our share of weakness and proclivity to sin and failure. The more honest we become with ourselves, the more free we are to admit it.

We are told to "be perfect just as your heavenly Father is perfect" (Matt. 5:4–7), but that does not mean we can never struggle in this life. In fact, the Scriptures are very clear that we *will* struggle. Perhaps what we need is a new perspective with which to look at our pain. We need to accept that some of us have certain weaknesses that may take significant time to work through, perhaps even a lifetime. I like to call these weaknesses "buttons."

The Lord continues to try and help me identify those buttons and what triggers them. Much of my growth in the Lord has been a process of either eliminating those weaknesses or minimizing their negative effects. After long, difficult battles, I now realize that some of them will go away and some won't. The trick for me is realizing what they are, where they are, and what triggers them, and then surrounding myself with the proper people and disciplines so that the impact they have is healthy instead of destructive. Maybe it is time to rethink this subject of woundedness, examining weakness as it is transformed by the power of Christ's resurrection.

From Woundedness to Glory

What will we look like in our resurrected bodies? We have probably all thought about this at one time or another. Obviously all we can do is speculate, but I wonder if our idea of redemption is accurate. Often when we think of the resurrected body, we think of some pristine image that is too aesthetically brilliant for the human eye. Perhaps we will look like this, but do we leave room for the possibility of the resurrection being nothing like what we might imagine? After all, St. Paul tells us that "eye has not seen, and ear has not heard . . . what God has prepared for those who love him" (1 Cor. 5). I wonder if our concept of glorification and perfection need redemption so desperately that, when we are before Him and we see Him as He is, our whole understanding will change!

We only know of one resurrected body—Jesus Christ—and His body has wounds in it. Isn't it something that in His resurrected body, His wounds were still there? Of course, the primary reason for Christ's wounds is our salvation. He was broken that we might be healed. He took upon Himself the woundedness of us all, became bruised for the penalty of our sin. We cherish the wounds of Christ because they have purchased our freedom.

I would suggest, however, that perhaps there is something else here for us all, a more personal corollary. Sometimes our own wounds and weaknesses, our own struggles are the very tools that God uses to manifest Himself in our lives. Perhaps some of those wounds will be the very things we treasure because they have helped us become more like Jesus, to identify with Him, to look like Him. They have helped us to grow in holiness. They have helped us to move from pride and arrogance to humility. They have helped us to become compassionate, empathetic, and able to identify with those who are weak. They have enabled us to grow in being able to forgive and to love as Jesus loved. Our woundedness can do this. Ironically the pain that we fear can actually become the very agent of transformation when an honest Christian believer is open and humble about them as well as repentant when those wounds hurt others.

Teresa of Avila often prayed to be Christ to the world, to be the Lord's hands and feet. I have reflected on this many times, and each time I have a similar thought. The hands and feet of Jesus were wounded. If we desire to be transformed into His image, we need to ask ourselves what it means to be a wounded foot, or a wounded hand, or a bleeding head. How much are we ready to suffer for our sin and the sin of the world?

Who knows—maybe when the last trumpet sounds, those millions and millions of glorified bodies will be adorned with glorified wounds, wounds that on earth were joined with the five wounds of the Son of God and became the very agents of change and transformation in the Christian life.

In a certain way we may almost boast of our wounds as we are told in 2 Corinthians 11: "If I must boast, I will boast of the things that show my weakness." These are the words of a very mature Paul who understood woundedness and weakness with great clarity and depth. Paul is somewhat of an authority on the subject; he had gone through it all, in and out of struggle and rejection and the purifying fire—a complete believer who understood his own weakness.

When Paul wrote to the Corinthians, he responded to people who questioned his apostolic authority. Interestingly Paul defends his authority on the basis of his own weaknesses. He talks to the Corinthians about his handwriting and how frail it is, about his physical weakness, about his thorn in the flesh and his struggles. In 2 Corinthians 12:7, Paul tells the Corinthians, "to keep me from becoming conceited because of these surpassingly great revelations, there was given to me a thorn in the flesh, a messenger of Satan to torment me."

St. Paul pleaded with the Lord to take away his thorn, and there is absolutely nothing wrong with asking the Lord to take away pain. But God did not answer Paul the way he in his humanness would have liked. God chose a bigger yes for Paul. He said, "My grace is sufficient for you, for power is made perfect in weakness" (2 Cor. 12:9). Then he transformed the thorn and used it to exact holiness from his servant. Paul responded, "I will boast all the more gladly about my weakness, so that Christ's power may rest on me. That is why, for Christ's sake, I delight in my weakness, in insults, in hardships, in persecutions, in difficulties. For when I am weak, then I am strong" (2 Cor. 12:10 NIV).

What a marvelous lesson for us all. Paul, a major leader of the Church, boasts not first about his spiritual revelations nor about his anointing or call, but rather about his sufferings, his struggles, his being left for dead, his being misunderstood, his struggle and burden for the churches, his wounds, his weaknesses, his difficulties over the years, and the incredible grace of God that was always with him.

Paul understood what it means to embrace the cross of Jesus Christ. He allowed Christ to be his strength and his sufficiency. That same Jesus is the one whom we serve, and He says the same to us. "My grace is sufficient for you, for power is made perfect in weakness" (2 Cor. 12:9).

The same principle can be applied to your family and mine. In our family's weakness, Christ's power is perfected. Only when we are in touch with our weakness and humbled about it can God's power break into and transform our lives. When we deny our weakness, we try to stand on our own strength. When we admit weakness, we can then beg for the *Lord's* strength to uphold us. That same strength, in turn, prepares us to become vessels of mercy ourselves. So we are changed, and we bear fruit in our compassion to others.

Bishop Sheen: Overcoming Fear of the Cross

In his marvelous autobiography, *Treasure in Clay,* Bishop Fulton Sheen, one of the heroes of the faith, discusses the stages of his own life, one of which he calls "staurophobia" or "fear of the cross." He examines the powerful confrontation between Christ and Peter in the New Testament. We all know the moment. It is recorded in Matthew 16, an intense experience of the highs and the lows for Simon Peter. (Does that sound like anyone you know?) Peter had just earned the Lord's blessing because when asked, "Who do you say that I am," only Peter replied clearly, "You are the Messiah, the Son of the living God" (Matt. 16:16). For that response, Jesus affirmed Peter with those marvelous words, "Blessed are you, Simon son of Jonah. For flesh and blood has not revealed this to you, but my heavenly Father" (Matt. 16:17). He also commissioned Peter for the special task of leadership in the church.

Yet on the heels of that glorious event, Peter receives stern correction. Jesus began to teach the disciples the meatier things; He told them of his suffering and death. And we read in the words of the Gospel writer, "Peter took him aside and began to rebuke him, 'God forbid, Lord! No such thing shall ever happen to you.'" (Matt. 16:22). But Jesus turned to Peter and responded, "Get behind me, Satan!" (Matt. 16:22). Bishop Fulton Sheen tells us, "The reaction of our Lord was like a thunderbolt."[1]

He then reflects upon his own imitation of Peter in this fear of the cross, realizing that, like Peter, he wanted to avoid the suffering too. Finally he shares with all of us with tremendous honesty, an event that occurred in his later years. The occasion, open-heart surgery. Read the words of this great apostle of the faith.

God does not like unfinished symphonies or unfurled flags. In His mercy He will finish the temple we have left unfinished and clean and polish that which has remained unadorned. What we may regard as an evil may be actually a hidden good like the surgeon's use of a scalpel. He does not ask us if we will accept the finishing of the work His Father sent Him to do. He drafts us in to His service as Simon the Cyrene that we might not be unripe and unplucked wheat in His Eucharistic sanctuary. He has many ways of tightening the violin strings that the priesthood may give forth a better harmony.

Since I would not take up the Cross, the Lord would lay it on my back as He laid it on Simon of Cyrene, who later came to love it. The cross took two forms: trial inside the Church and outside the Church. Eventually I came to see that the Lord was teaching me not only to be a priest, but also to be a victim. This explains why two of the books I authored are on this very subject.

I can remember, when, after four months in the hospital, I began to recover; I was reading Mass on an altar constructed over the bed before a few priests and friends. I spontaneously gave a sermon, which I remember so well. I said that I was glad that I had open-heart surgery because when the Lord comes to take us all, He will look to see if we have any marks of the Cross upon ourselves. He will look at our hands to see if they are crucified from sacrificial giving; He will look at our feet to see if they have been thorn-bruised and nail-pierced searching for lost sheep; He will look at our heart to see if that has been opened to receive His Divine Heart. Oh, what joy is mine just to have endured the minuscule imitation of His suffering on the cross by having a wounded side. Maybe He will recognize me from that scar and receive me into His kingdom.[2]

Bishop Sheen and I are referring to redemptive suffering, not fruitless pain. We all ache from some pain, but it is not the pain in and of itself that purifies. Purification and transformation come to the degree that we choose to unite our wounds with Christ and ultimately begin to become more like Christ.

How does this happen? God allows us thorns in the flesh, but as with Paul, He can also turn those very thorns into the vehicles of our own holiness, and therefore we can boast about them because they make us look more like Christ. In our woundedness, He forges His very image; His wounded imprint is sealed upon us. Again, embracing our woundedness can be a powerful step toward the fullness of our salvation, and until we reach that final day, we are seeking continual, dynamic transformation in Christ, to become more like Him every day, to be transformed from glory to glory (2 Cor. 3:18).

In the first letter of John we read, "What we shall be has not yet been revealed. We do know that when it is revealed we shall be like him, for we shall see him as he is" (1 John 3:2). If we are being transformed from glory to glory, then we are gradually beginning to look, act, and react more like Christ. If we continue on earth to daily move and grow in God's presence, we will (at the beatific vision) in a certain sense be like God.

That is overwhelming. We're not there yet, and the only way we can get there is through this inner transformation and purification, a dynamic process that, more often than not, occurs through struggle and difficulty, weakness and frailty.

Similarly our families are all suffering in some way. God has allowed that suffering to purify our families and make them holy. Just as personal suffering allows us "to look more like Christ," so corporate suffering in the family allows us to look more like the church." Many of the Christian communities of the early church struggled with serious sin and weakness—sexual immorality, idolatry, and so on. In particular, the Corinthian community struggled, but they were still called to be the Church. Their struggle was the main reason Paul wrote about the thorn in his flesh. He encouraged the church to turn from that weakness by God's power and offer all the glory to God.

Our victory over struggle glorifies the Lord. Each time we rely on God's power to smother any breath of temptation, we allow Him deeper into our being. Evil is edged out; God fills its place. As Christians awaiting the beatific vision, we want to step into this process and grow. As families, we need to grab hold of this vision if we are to be transformed into the domestic church.

Response to Suffering

If we don't have any room in our theology for this kind of redemptive suffering, for this approach to dealing with weakness, we may become confused or, worse, cynical because our problems and struggles generally do not disappear. They may intensify, decrease, or change in form, but they don't often disappear. Instead of expecting or waiting for our pain to vanish, we need to change our response and begin to deal with it.

One temptation that we all deal with when confronted with weakness is a naivete about what it means to call upon God's power. We say, "I can do all things through Christ who strengthens me" (Phil. 4:13 NKJV). I can do *all things*—what does that mean? Sometimes with a certain false bravado, we can pretend that we don't experience or shouldn't experience problems as a Christian family. But victory in Jesus does not mean we sail through life trouble free; it means that we get in touch with our inner wounds and deal with them by His grace. It means that as a body we call upon God's strength, wisdom, and power to raise us up through the struggle and to allow that weakness to become the very thing about us that most glorifies our Father.

Pretending that problems don't exist is called "denial." Denial blocks healing. Even if they seem to disappear, those same problems will resurface in some form or other. Christian families, especially, often feel ashamed to admit struggle. But just because some or all of our family members are baptized, committed, and faithful followers of Christ does not mean struggles in the family disappear. Yes, we are new creations in Christ and can daily be recreated. We have changed internally, what we value has changed, and what we hold onto and treasure has changed. But we still live in a fallen world and will experience struggle. The key is to admit the struggle and be freed of it.

Another mistake is to nurture a defeatist attitude ("I can't do anything about my weakness; that's just the way I am, and people should accept me the way I am"). It is true that we all have a God-given, natural personality with certain flaws. It is also true that our families have a corporate personality with certain defects. But the greater spiritual truth is that God's grace builds on nature. Therefore, through our response to God's power, we can bring under submission unhealthy behavior patterns that block God's healing of our wounds.

But our response is the key. We need to learn to own and personalize our strengths and weaknesses and take responsibility for our behaviors. As families, we need to talk about our struggles, listen to one another, and work together toward healthy alternatives.

Joyful Perseverance

The apostle James tells us to "consider it all joy, my brothers, when you encounter various trials" (James 1:2). The healthy Christian family perseveres in trials, and even counts them as pure joy, knowing that God desires only for the family what is truly best. Healthy families realize that in all struggle, God will eventually bring about a complete reorganization or their behavior patterns, responses, values, life-style, and perceptions—all because He is faithful in granting the holy desire of becoming church. Our families will experience continual change and should be open to this without harboring a sense of failure. We must focus on our faithfulness to God's call.

Our wounds may not go away, at least not for a long time. Let's allow them to sanctify us and our families. In our woundedness, we can find the blessed hope of eternal glory. Paul wrote to the Roman Christians:

I consider that the sufferings of this present time are as nothing compared with the glory to be revealed for us. . . . We know that all creation is groaning in labor pains even until now; and not only that, but we ourselves, who have the firstfruits of the Spirit. . . . We know that all things work for good for those who love God, who are called according to his purpose. (Rom. 8:18, 22–23, 28)

God's purpose for the Christian family is to be the domestic church, the church in the home. The call to be church carries with it trial and suffering. It has from the beginning. But for all those called according to this purpose, God will be faithful and strengthen them for all eternity.

You see, He has always chosen the wounded and the lame. Why? So that He can reveal His marvelous glory. Rather than run from the pain, perhaps it is time for us to turn around. After all, that's what the word *conversion* means in Greek, to "turn around." Maybe we have looked at this whole issue of pain and suffering the wrong way for a long time. Maybe we need a deeper conversion, a conversion that can only come through a deeper devotion. That's what we'll examine next—true devotion for the domestic church.

6

True Devotion

What comes to mind when you hear the word *devotion?* Often the word conjures up any number of actions that we learned at home or Sunday school. Perhaps you think of a church building. Or Dad or Mom's leading the family in prayer after dinner. Or if you are from a liturgical church, the marvelous "private devotions" such as stations of the cross or a form prayer associated with special family events.

For many, these types of devotions carry with them a certain security. We know that when we pray this way, we are doing something specifically with God in mind. Devotions are good and holy activities because they can bring us closer to the Lord. Certainly all devotions must be kept in perspective and appreciated for what they are. As with anything else in the Christian life, balance is critical. If we emphasize them too much or too little, we can destroy their authentic power to change us and their function as tremendous instruments of prayer. But they are only the entryway to an intimate relationship with God.

Prayer. Prayer of the heart is the goal, not the structure of the devotion itself. The form of devotion, in and of itself, is not holy. Reciting prayers is not necessarily holy. Reading the Bible is not holy. Not even the action of attending a church function can bring us closer to God in and of itself.

Devotions can be empty without an accompanying interior relationship and motivation of love for God. We should want all that we do, be it holy devotions or everyday duties, to direct us more deeply into the heart of Christ. Devotions are a fruit of the internal movement of being devoted to God.

Yet *devotions* and *devotion* are two very different things. Devotions involve action; devotion is a love relationship. The heart of the believer and his or her motives make the action holy. We should, however, always practice such devotions with an awareness that there is a danger of becoming dependent or subservient to the form of the devotion instead of the One to whom the devotion is directed.

The opposite danger exists as well, the danger of being a full-blooded "interior" Christian. These people have no room in their spirituality for pious practices. In fact, some even view devotions as a subtle form of idolatry. For instance, many who do not agree with or possibly do not understand Mary's ongoing motherly role for Christians can believe that when Catholics honor her, or honor any of the saints for that matter, they are somehow detracting from worship of God. Yet true Marian devotion, like any other devotion, directs us only to God or it is false. He alone is the goal of all our devotion.

Instead of criticizing certain devotions, we should first try to understand them and then take full advantage of those that through our own meditation allow us a glimpse of the spiritual mysteries of God. Devotions are signs that point us toward heaven.

Human beings need signs to help us on some level understand the supernatural. God knew that. That is why when on earth, Christ consistently performed visible miracles—to help us understand! He didn't need to prove anything to himself. He did it for our benefit. In a certain sense, the same is true with devotions. In their tangibility, they help us to grasp in some visible form mysteries that we can never understand on their deepest levels.

Devotion is one of the critical elements that brings the domestic church to life. It allows the structure of the sacred to find a place in what is so often experienced as secular. Like leaven in the loaf, devotion if sprinkled throughout the life of the Christian family raises it to become the domestic church.

What Is Devotion?

Devotion in the Christian sense has been defined by Thomas Aquinas as "being dedicated or vowed to God's service" or a "ready willingness in giving oneself up to service in God's household." Further it is not an unusual virtue, but a primary one in the faith. A primary quality? What does that mean? Maybe one aspect of what it means is that true devotion is the heart of religion, the crowning accomplishment. The "service in God's household" to which the saint points is first service where "the rubber meets the road," in the domestic church of the family. After all, it is there that service to the extended household, the Church, is learned and finds its first expression.

Being devoted to God as a Christian family means being ready at all times to serve God's household by serving our own household. Like Thomas, we should not see devotion as an extraordinary virtue, but as a quality of daily living. Our lives are to be directed to the service of God. And what's the best way to serve God? To be faithful to His call on our lives. The best way for families to serve God is to understand love of God as the root of all activity in the domestic church.

One common mistake is to believe that devotion is a call for only certain people, those who can spend long hours in prayer and meditation. In my tradition as a Catholic Christian, this translates to the religious life. By "religious life" Catholics refer to monks, nuns, priests, and others especially given to service. But living a life of devotion does not exclusively belong to the domain of vowed religious men and women or to ordained ministers. Certainly to some extent, the lives of priests, ministers, brothers, sisters, and nuns are often structured for more formal time in prayer and in service to God's church. They are free to pursue God wholeheartedly in everything they do. Paul realized this even in the early church:

I should like you to be free of anxieties. An unmarried man is
anxious about the things of the Lord, how he may please the Lord.
But a married man is anxious about the things of the world, how
he may please his wife, and he is divided. An unmarried woman or
a virgin is anxious about the things of the Lord, so that she may
be holy in both body and spirit. A married woman, on the other
hand, is anxious about the things of the world, how she may
please her husband. (1 Cor. 7:32–34)

Obviously Paul was writing from a deep sense of urgency as he
looked toward the *parousia*. Nearly two thousand years later, his
point, however, is still well taken. Family life, if we allow it, *can*
distract us from the ultimate end of being focused on God.

Yet families are to be no less devoted to God than the single or
celibate person. Whatever our role in the Body of Christ, we are
to direct our primary attention to God. As families, our primary
goal should not be getting the kids through college, teaching
them how to be successful, being content when they are married
or secure in a job. The first goal is to teach them right now single-
hearted loyalty and faithfulness to God and to practice living that
as a family. The goal is true devotion.

Francis de Sales, in his book *Introduction to the Devout Life*,
lays out a basic description of devotion toward which we can all
strive. He says,

In as much as our love exchange with God strengthens us to do
good, it is called charity. When it has reached the degree of
perfection at which it not only makes us do good but also do this
carefully, frequently, and promptly, it is called devotion . . . charity
and devotion differ no more from one another than does flame
from the fire. Charity is spiritual fire, and when it bursts into
flames, it is called devotion.[1]

What does this mean? De Sales starts by explaining that God
has gifted us with an organic need to love and be loved. That's

why family life is so important. It is meant to be the key place to express and experience unconditional love. Unfortunately this is often not the case. So God mercifully offers His love through friends, church members, co-workers, and most powerfully through a one-on-one relationship with Him. When we respond to God's love (through any of these vehicles), that love strengthens us to do good and we grow in even greater love. We are built up in the virtue of charity.

We don't, however, always choose to RSVP God's invitation of love. So many times we become impatient, angry, or self-centered, particularly in the home. Isn't it strange how we often treat with the least care and respect those whom we love the most? Growing in charity is, I believe, the most difficult task for the family. We should never stop trying, though.

De Sales suggests that charity can actually reach a degree of perfection. That does not mean we no longer need to grow in love. However, it does mean that our approach to charity at some point takes on a new dimension. Doing good actually becomes a habit, in a certain sense. We don't just treat our mother nicely because it's Mother's Day or do something for our son because it's his birthday. We love not so much in the special moments, but in the ordinary happenings in the home. We begin to respond in all situations in a loving way. That response is continually perfected and eventually becomes devotion. Charity in its perfection is devotion.

Some of you may be wondering that if charity is the greatest gift (1 Cor. 13), how can we say that the perfection of charity is devotion? The distinction must be made between the *gift* of charity given to us by God and the *response* to that gift, which involves our choice to cooperate with that gift. If we choose to build on that gift, we can attain true devotion. What allows us to make this choice? It goes back to the simple beginning of being wholly directed toward God—loving Him, loving His people, loving His plan for my family. After all, in the words of the beloved disciple, John, "God is love."

The Proper Perspective

True devotion? The modern culture invites us to be devoted to everything *but* God. We attach our affections and sometimes our entire selves to many things of the world.

Let's take a moment and consider what occupies most of our time and thought. Does our family take time to talk to God or think about Him? Or is our family time spent in front of the TV? Fathers, do we, without requirement, consistently surrender family time to a job? Mothers, is your hobby keeping you out of the house several days a week? Kids, are your friends more important than your family life? Recreation, jobs, hobbies, friends—we can actually be devoted to these things in an unhealthy way. We can and should be committed to these things, but excessive commitment is inappropriate. Commitment is proper to people. Devotion is proper only to God.

We all become absorbed in activities now and then, but is our focus consistently out of God's order? We should constantly examine and reexamine this because it's so easy to lose focus. A good measuring stick to answer this question of priorities is always to look at the fruits of our lives. If we're honest, a close inspection reveals that much of our time is spent on empty behaviors, fillers of our time, activities that do not flow from our primary devotion to God. These will not build up our families. Nor will they mold our families into the domestic church that God wants us to be.

My family has tried different ways of fostering devotion to God. We have not always been consistent, and we regularly have to adjust for ages, responsibilities, and schedules. We find a continual challenge in balancing devotion, discipline, refreshment, leisure, and fun. When my children were much younger, we considered various approaches to the recreational use of television. We lived in a very large old home that had a dark dungeon-like basement when we moved in. We remodeled it into a family room that also became a family prayer room. We placed a large cross in the center of the wall, moved the sofa around, and hung pictures that reflected our faith.

Everything fit except the television. We owned a large twenty-five-inch console. No matter where it was placed in a room, it became the focus of attention, even when it was not turned on. Laurine once said, "The television is like an altar in this home." We noticed that during family prayers all eyes, little and big, were drawn to the television. So one day we said, "Why not make it a family altar?" So we did. We covered it with a cloth when not in use and placed a Bible on it.

We then began to practice, in a more disciplined fashion than before, regular morning and evening prayers as a family before the cross and the "altar." We placed things on the altar that would enrich our family prayer, instead of taking away from it. The day the television became an altar in our home was a significant day for us as a family because it provided a springboard for a richer family worship time. It stood as a symbol of the centrality of what our true devotion could be as a family. This change greatly enhanced our life as the domestic church, but eventually it became unworkable and unrealistic.

Every time I recall this story, it challenges me to evaluate my life and my family's life. I ask the question "Do I have the right kind of devotion, and does my family have the right kind of devotion?" We still have a family altar, though over the years the television has been moved. The altar is now the mantle over our fireplace with a cross on it, and it is the first thing you see when you come into our home. It stands as a challenge to us of what is central to our family life, true devotion to Jesus Christ.

True devotion is a must for our families, but it is also a process of changes throughout our lives. We can always grow in devotion, just as we can always grow in love of God. The moment we think we have reduced it to a perfect formula, though, we are probably farther from the mark. It's not about a formula, but a relationship that must continually be renewed with the Source and Summit of all true devotion, the Lord himself.

How to Foster True Devotion

True devotion can change our families; it allows us to reach the fullness of experience that God has planned for our life. But how "practical" is a life of devotion, a life of holiness in our world? That question reveals a fundamental confusion regarding the concept of practicality. As husbands, fathers, wives, and mothers, we do have a very real responsibility to care for our families, but we can never forget our primary responsibility to God. He has first called us to love, serve, and be devoted to Him and then to one another.

In the second letter of Peter, we find a beautiful message of encouragement: "His divine power has bestowed on us everything that makes for life and devotion, through the knowledge of him who called us by his own glory and power" (2 Peter 1:3). Through our knowledge of Jesus Christ who called us by His own glory and goodness, we have everything we need for a life of godliness, individually and as a family. Our families have been given the grace to reflect the life of God in the world and to be an image of Christ's love for His Church.

> For this very reason, make every effort to supplement your faith with virtue, virtue with knowledge, knowledge with self-control, self-control with endurance, endurance with devotion, devotion with mutual affection, mutual affection with love. If these are yours and increase in abundance, they will keep you from being idle or unfruitful in the knowledge of our Lord Jesus Christ. (2 Peter 1:5–8)

Peter tells all of us that we who walk under the banner of Christ as families should experience a certain kind of progression in holiness. This progression in holiness, this continual growth in love provides the foundation for true devotion. Family devotion is rooted in the practical experiences of family life. They provide the mortar for the whole structure.

Pope John Paul II speaks frequently about what he calls the

"universal call to holiness." Again, holiness is not something re-served for the few who have the privilege of being called to ex-traordinary vocations. No, the whole Church is called to holiness. Every Christian's vocation is true devotion, and Francis de Sales asserts that true devotion is possible in every vocation:

> In the creation, God commanded the plants to bring forth their fruits, each one after its own kind. So does he command all Christians, who are the living plants of His Church, to bring forth the fruits of devotion. Each according to his character and vocation. Devotion must be exercised in different ways by the gentleman, the workman, the servant, the prince, the widow, the maid, and the married woman. Not only this, but the practice of devotion must be adapted to the strength, the employment, and duties of everyone in particular. I ask you, Philothea [that's his disciple he is writing to], is it fit that a bishop should lead the solitary life of a Carthusian, or that married people should lay up a greater store of goods than the Capuchin? If a tradesman were to remain the whole day in church like a member of a religious order, or were a religious continually to be exposed to and encounter difficulties in the service of his neighbor, as a bishop is, would not such devotion be ridiculous, unorganized, and insupportable?
>
> Nevertheless, this fault is very common. . . . True devotion does no harm, but rather gives perfection to all things. When it goes contrary to our vocation, than without a doubt it is false.[2]

"The bee," said Aristotle, "extracts honey from flowers with-out injuring them, and leaves them as whole and fresh as when he found them." True devotion does even better. Not only does it not harm a vocation or even a job; rather it adorns and beautifies it. Every kind of precious stone receives a greater luster when cast into honey. Every vocation becomes more agreeable when united with true devotion. "The care of the family is rendered more peaceable, the love of the husband and wife more sincere, the service of the prince more faithful, and every type of employ-ment more pleasant and agreeable."[3]

All men, women, and children are called to holiness, and we

are called to encourage one another on to holiness, to bring our children into the life of holiness, and to make our homes places where the Lord would be comfortable. This requires us to be serious about a family life-style and spirituality oriented first toward God and then toward His people. Not so much a spirituality for lay people and families, but a true family and lay spirituality. An abiding presence of God in our homes, which transforms us.

Can My Family Be Devoted?

Sometimes it is difficult to see our families as holy, isn't it? Our children bicker with each other, or perhaps there is jealousy among them. We see them so engrossed in a sport that their entire lives revolve around it for a season. Some of our family members complain about going to church every Sunday. We think for certain that our family (especially the children) doesn't like religious talk, that our extended families may see us as unrealistic or fanatical, that our kids wouldn't be interested in spiritual things.

All of these may initially slow your family's transformation, but they need not be permanent barriers. Parents can combat all of those difficulties and more, one day at a time. We begin by correcting our children when they fail to treat each other in love. We gently and continually teach our children about priorities. We patiently bear with them when they struggle with doing the right thing. We believe in the goodness of our families and count on God's mercy to draw them closer to Him. We act as though the Lord is the Head of our family because He truly is.

Sometimes we fail to give children enough credit when talking about God. They are created for truth just as adults and should at least have the opportunity to respond to God. At the Franciscan University of Steubenville, where I used to work, we had two weekend conferences each summer geared specifically toward youth. Interestingly, of the dozen conferences offered, the high school youth and young adult conferences were the best attended by far. We literally had thousands of kids every summer responding to God's invitation for their lives. Kids are hungry for the gospel. As a father, those conferences always brought me great joy and hope for my own children and for the future of the Church.

All human beings, including children, have great potential to be in love with the Lord. As we know, however, the world is also attractive in all of its pomp and empty promises. Our families may not respond to God in the way we want them to, but persevering with them and praying for them is critical. They will respond because God is more invested in our children than we are. They ultimately belong to Him.

There may have to be quite a bit of change in our family—and hard work—but this is the reality of conversion. Dedicating our lives to God was a similar process for all of us. We had to make a decision to change our thinking, our actions, our reactions, everything. All of that change was and still is a painful process at times. Our fallen nature has a death grip on our lives, and being freed of that grip is a slow process. Similarly our families need to be fed truth and encouraged daily to live that truth. By word, example, and prayer, we patiently nourish that seed until it blossoms in splendor.

It may take many years before we see significant change in our family. Continue to fight the good fight of faith (1 Tim. 6:12). Be encouraged by holy families over the years who struggled with sin and abandonment to the world. One of the best-known and celebrated examples of patient endurance is Monica, the mother of Augustine, who pleaded with the Lord nearly twenty years for the conversion of her son. He did eventually convert and became wholeheartedly devoted to God. St. Augustine, set aflame by burning devotion to God, significantly changed the Church. His writings still do. Who knows? You may have another Augustine refusing to eat his string beans.

Devotion, Not Perfection

A life of holiness, a life of charity, a life of true devotion in the family is necessary for the domestic church. Marriage and family life is meant to be a path to heaven, another way of responding to the Master who says, "Deny yourself. Take up your cross and follow me" (see Matt. 16:24). We shoulder our crosses in the practical experiences of day-to-day life, putting aside our own desires and taking on God's desires, loving our spouse first and forgiving when we have been hurt, and loving our children by serving them. These are daily encounters that enable us to choose between self and God.

It may be intimidating, but we are called to "be perfect, as your heavenly Father is perfect" (Matt. 5:48). We cannot get around that passage if we are serious about Christian family life. I used to read that passage and say to myself, "I can't do it," because I thought Jesus was talking about perfectionism. Well, He's not.

What does it mean when Jesus calls His disciples (and, therefore, calls us) to be perfect? How do we do it? The Greek word for "perfect" is *telios,* which means "complete, mature, finished." For example, a hammer is *telios* when it is hammering a nail. A screwdriver is *telios* when it is turning a screw. A disciple is *telios* when he is living out his vocation to the best of his ability in the Lord.

A Christian family becomes *telios* as it grows into a domestic church. God wants husbands who are *telios* and truly "husbanding" their wives. He wants wives who are *telios* and living out their call as a full partner and participant, imitating Mary the mother of Jesus at the heart of the home. He desires children to be *telios,* loving and obeying their parents and growing to their full stature in the Lord.

Parents are called to enable, to equip, and to assist their children to live in perfect devotion and holiness. Husbands are called to assist their wives, and wives are called to assist their husbands. Together, as a family, we are called to move ahead toward perfection by cooperating with God in His work of making us like Jesus, the Perfect One.

Parents can begin by praying for a greater desire for personal holiness and devotion. Example is always a great witness. Get excited about God with your children. Draw them into your joy. Children most often use their parents as the primary role model, so we have to give them something positive to imitate.

Setting a good example is vital, but instructing our children is no less important. So crucial is the teaching role of parents that I have devoted the next entire chapter to it. For the moment, suffice it to say that human beings are creatures of habit. This goes double for children. Children mimic what they see and hear. Unfortunately many adults seeking to set an example for children have been exposed to much ugliness as a child and, therefore, have developed negative thought and behavior patterns because of their experience. Admitting and dealing with this reality has given birth to an entire movement in our society of "Adult Children." There are Adult Children of Alcoholics groups and others multiplying rapidly. As the term implies, people in these groups acknowledge the negative impact their childhood has had on their own personal formation. For many, the "survival" or "coping" mechanisms they developed as children have become patterns of self-destruction and sources of pain in their adult life.

Perhaps an adult struggled unconsciously for many years with a feeling of deprivation because he or she did not receive enough positive affirmation as a child. In order to cope, he or she may have developed some destructive habits such as bingeing on food or abusing alcohol. Others may constantly instigate arguments in their thirst for attention. Still others may nurture and hide depression by avoiding the rest of the family or refusing to share their intimate lives. All of these behaviors have deep emotional roots and can in fact develop into negative addictions. If not confronted, one can sustain this behavior for a lifetime. Our own negative addictions often cause the greatest problem as we parents seek to raise our children with love and devotion for the Lord.

But there is *good news!* The good news is the gospel of Jesus Christ, a gospel that saves on increasingly deeper levels. Like a burning torch, God's healing light pierces the darkness of our fear, pain, and guilt. The light of Christ is our freedom, placing life and hope where there once was only death and destruction. Hope springs eternal. That hope, the Scripture says, will "not disappoint [us], because the love of God has been poured out into our hearts" (Rom. 5:5). Based on that hope, and with confidence in the good news, we must remember that positive behavior patterns can change our personal lives and, of course, the lives of our children.

There are many positive habits to share with our children. We can teach them, for instance, to approach their own bodies as "temple[s] of the holy Spirit" (1 Cor. 6:19) and, therefore, to take proper stewardship over those bodies by eating properly and exercising. If we are able to instill this in their formative years, it will stand the test of time. Encouraging them to form good study habits and patterns of daily living are indispensable gifts that we can give to them as parents in their early years.

Well, how much more important is it for us to give them food that will endure beyond the tomb, spiritual food? "If you then, who are wicked, know how to give good gifts to your children, how much more will your heavenly Father give good things to those who ask him" (Matt. 7:11).

What is that food? The spiritual life! The spiritual disciplines! Imparting to our children a healthy responsibility for their own lives is one of the greatest gifts we can pass on to them. Indeed, such a heritage will endure and will bear fruit for years to come. Encouraging them to be responsible for a daily time of prayer, showing and affirming true devotion in their own personal lives, modeling that kind of devotional practice within the home—these habits of holiness will last for all time.

Maybe you are reading this, and rather than being encouraged, you feel despair. Perhaps, for example, your children are in their later teens. You wish you had it to do all over again, but you don't. Again, there is hope. The power of God far exceeds anything we can ask for or imagine. His mercy is timeless. Never underestimate His ability to make up for our own deficiencies and His desire to bring success into the midst of our failures. Remember, no matter what you did, they are *His* children first and foremost. He claimed them through baptism. Rededicate your children now. Watch His miraculous intervention in their lives. Have hope.

Our Christian history is full of examples of living hope. I like to call them the "surprises of the Spirit." Monica of Hippo, whom I mentioned earlier, was one such example. A devoted mother, she watched her son, Augustine, live a reckless life. Augustine was the stereotypical "party animal." His cavalier attitude and desire for draining the gusto out of life left little room for his mother's devotion. Monica did not give up. She prayed. She prayed more. And she never ceased praying. In the end, nearly twenty years of intercessory prayer by a devoted mother not only freed the hand of God to bring about the conversion of her son, but prompted God to unleash in Augustine's life the kind of spiritual power and authority that would catapult him into significant leadership as the Bishop of Hippo. His leadership did not end with Hippo but affected the entire Church and to this day has affected each of our lives. This Augustine of Hippo is St. Augustine of Christian fame, the one whose writings (such as *City of God* and *The Confessions*) have influenced the way all believers view our own personal lives, the role of the Church, and the world. Do not underestimate God's love for your children. They are His children first.

Achieving Devotion in Our Families

How do we achieve this devotion? This may sound like an overly simplistic answer, but nonetheless it is true: We do it by taking prayer seriously. We ought to pray as families and as individuals. We should encourage our children to pray. We should hold up heroes of the faith as models for our children, men and women who challenge them to lives of purity and faithfulness to God. We should regularly embrace the gifts of special grace available to us in the life of our church. We need to take His promises to heart. We need to take His Word found in the Scripture seriously, to read it and love it, to pore through it and be formed by it. We need to cooperate with His grace in every vehicle that He uses. And we need to begin to be committed to each other with the steadfast commitment of Christ.

This kind of devoted, ardent, familial commitment is demonstrated in the lives of many saints and Christian leaders throughout the ages and in all Christian traditions. Children need heroes and models, people they can look up to. If we are serious about raising holy children, then we need to reject many of the models the contemporary age holds up for them. They are not heroes, but often antiheroes. We need to magnify instead models of the faith, truly steeped in virtue, piety, and courage.

I have always found the women saints in my own Catholic Christian tradition particularly inspiring. For example, Elizabeth of Hungary was a wife and mother who raised three children. But she went beyond her home and expanded her mothering to take in the poor and the orphaned, the sick and the dying. She built hospices and refuges for them, and when they filled up, she brought them into her own home. Elizabeth, in the context of her family, learned to work out her own salvation and lead others to Christ. She was devoted to God first, and she used all of the grace stored in the treasure of her family to do the work that God had for her.

Not all of us are expected to die a martyr's death, take the dying into our homes, or raise nineteen children, but we are all called to the pursuit of Christian virtue in our particular situation. If we study the many holy examples within our Christian tradition, if we root ourselves in the gospel of Christ, if as families we live out our call to be the domestic church, we can have a great impact on the world around us. So often what we find in our day, and perhaps even experience ourselves, is conversion to a world system that has squeezed out God. We often give in to the system instead of being the light and leaven, the salt, and the hope for this difficult age. It is time to raise a standard of family life which, though perceived as counter-cultural, can and will change the world.

Husbands, we should have as our goal becoming like Jesus: men of prayer; men of compassion, love, and mercy; men of justice, holiness, and devotion. Not only should we read the Scriptures and pray, but we should also lead our families to do the same. Christian wives should first be women of God, taking as their models Mary (the mother of Jesus) and all the holy women through the ages. Be the woman that God wants you to be, a disciple of His, a sister to your husband, and a mother to God's children.

Children, as well, are called to holiness and sanctity. They are called to take their rightful place in the domestic church of the home, serving, loving, and growing. They are called to true devotion, taking as their example holy children throughout the ages who have said yes to Jesus Christ. Sometimes we think we shouldn't expect children to live holy lives. We are wrong. Children are called—and by the grace of their baptism empowered—to live holy lives.

There is not only a place in the Church, but a desperate need for such holy families. As with the whole Church, the domestic church is strengthened, empowered, and animated by the devotion of her members. Remember, "when the fullness of time had come" (Gal. 4:4), God gave the world a sign on earth of the truths of heaven. He did so by being born of a woman into a family. There the Son of God allowed Himself, in His humanity, to be instructed and to grow in wisdom and stature (Luke 2:52). Don't underestimate what He desires to do in the midst of your family. He may not be present in the flesh, but He is profoundly present in Spirit. Make room for Him through a family life in which He is enthroned by true devotion.

Remember that the incarnation is an ever-present mystery. God became flesh. "The Word [of God] became flesh and made his dwelling among us" and we beheld His glory (John 1:14). The Word of God still dwells among us as He manifests Himself through the Church. Its most vital cell is the domestic church, Christian family life. We are called to live a supernatural home life where Jesus Christ is manifested. This manifestation or "epiphany" of the Lord will be in direct proportion to our decision to give him room in the manger of our homes. Devotion is like the yeast that will make the whole loaf rise. It is like the eggs in the cake batter. It works itself through and manifests itself in every aspect of our life. Our devotion will be present not only when we are saying prayers but when we are playing, loving, serving, resting, and just plain living. After all, that is one of the most beautiful things about the Christian message. God entered into the whole of the human experience. He desires to enter into the whole of your family experience if you will let Him in.

7

Apostolic Instruction

One Sunday in early spring, several years ago, our family decided to go on a picnic. We had just returned from church and we all wanted to celebrate. It was one of those rare days where everyone was in a great mood, the sky was brilliant blue, and the sun was shining as bright as I ever remember. We just had to be outside on such a perfect day, so we headed to a nearby favorite spot in the beautiful hills of West Virginia. We stopped at a picnic area, ate our lunch, and while Laurine played with our infant son, Joel, I threw the frisbee with our three eldest.

After some time, I noticed that our fourth child, MaryEllen, had wandered over the hill and was picking dandelions, which she maintains are the most beautiful flowers that grow. Of course, until that morning I thought they were a weed, but the simple insights of a child are heartwarming, aren't they? We all eventually joined her, roaming through the meadow, drinking deeply of the beauty of the hillside and drawing strength from this obvious display of God's presence in the world. The children were frantically picking the wild flowers that adorned the hillside. Eventually they bound together all of their pickings in one bunch and presented the bouquet to their mom.

My son Keith then remembered a story about four-leaf clovers and good luck and leprechauns. He became increasingly excited as he talked and finally bounded back into the meadow in search of his very own four-leaf clover. Of course the rest of the kids followed. One by one, they returned to the huge picnic blanket claiming that they had found a four-leaf clover. I knew that probably none of them had, so I told them a story that gave the ordinary clover a special charm.

I held up a clover for them to see and asked two questions: "How many clovers do I have?" and "How many leaves does it have?" The responses were one and three respectively. I then explained to them how a bishop named Patrick had once explained the Trinity to the Irish people with just such a clover. Did my children understand the intellectual underpinnings of the theology of the Trinity? I doubt it. Great theologians have tried through the ages to clarify this mystery to no avail. But it was a healthy start. Using the natural stuff of daily life to convey supernatural truth—that is what parental instruction is all about.

Parents are meant to be vessels for their children's salvation, imparting to them the truths of the faith. One way we do that is by teaching. We are called to instruct our children in the faith. The role of teacher is a very critical role and one that isn't understood or talked about as much as it should be, but being the first teachers of our children is actually our primary vocation as parents.

John Paul II states that,

> For Christian parents the mission to educate, a mission rooted as we have said in their participation in God's creating activity, has a new specific source in the Sacrament of Marriage, which consecrates them for the strictly Christian education of their children.[1]

That does not mean we leave the education of our children to the schools or to the Sunday school teachers. It means we as parents have been given the means to be the main educators of our children. In marriage we are set apart. As mothers and fathers we are set apart to educate our children.

The book of Judges contains a story that I believe speaks to all parents and their responsibility to their children. The story is of

101

Manoah and his wife and an angel's prediction of their offspring. Upon hearing the news, Manoah prayed that God would send the angel to instruct him as to how to care for the child. God did send the angel, and Manoah petitioned him saying, "How shall we order the child? And how shall we do unto him?" (Judges 13:12).

Andrew Murray reflects deeply on this Scripture in his book *How To Raise Your Children for Christ.* In his unique perception, he is touched by Manoah's abiding sense of holy responsibility in the training of his child.[2] Murray points to Manoah's humility, a man not necessarily trusting his own ability, but desiring God's full wisdom. He suggests that this approach to parenthood is

> quite a contrast to the thoughtless self-confidence with which many Christian parents undertake the training of their children. How little effort is made to realize the importance and solemnity of the work! How little real prayer for the preparation of the Spirit to fit them for it! How little surrender to a life for God.[3]

Isn't this what is necessary for our families—reverence for the task of parenthood, prayer, and surrender? Writers on the family agree that the ideas and behaviors formulated in the first seven years are often permanent values.[4] Parents need to utilize that time in the best way. Teach them truth. Guide them toward everlasting life.[5]

Clearly we are responsible for our children's instruction, but how do we go about doing this? We must present to our children the truth of life, the truth of God. These are mysteries that cannot be grasped through verbal teaching alone. They must become a way of life. If they are a way of life for parents, the home will become the sacred school it is meant to be. Words can never be the only method of expression of our faith. We must also teach through the example of our lives.

To teach our children with authority, we parents must first know the teaching in our own hearts. We must know what it means to live as baptized Christians, that we have submerged the old man and have emerged from the living waters as new creations. We need to know that we are full members of God's family and have been given the gift of eternally belonging to that family. We hope we have cultivated our relationship with the Lord and know His intimacy. These are the truths with which we nurture our children, and if we live them from the heart, our children will be affected. So we must live our faith fervently, lovingly, and consistently before it will mean anything to our children. The holiness of our own lives and the openness of our love for God will spill over to them.

My early childhood memories are filled with people who truly loved God. My first-grade teacher, Sister William Patricia, talked about Jesus as though He were her best friend. She told me I could do the same, and I did. Although I wandered from the faith as a teenager, I later came home to the Church. Her open witness to God had a great deal to do with it.

My grandmother Ida was also a woman of great faith. At age seventeen, when I returned to the Lord, I went to tell my grandmother about my new faith. She hugged me tightly and wept. "If you only knew," she said, "how many years I've prayed for you!"

Their lives, and many others, have shaped my faith, and I am grateful for their examples. This is what parenting is all about.

Teach Them with Words

Deuteronomy 6 directs parents to teach their children about the law of God. "These commandments," says the Lord, "I give to you today are to be upon your hearts. Impress them on your children." We are not to be just casually talking about them or bringing them up on Sunday in the privacy of our home. The Scripture reads:

> Speak of them at home and abroad, whether you are busy or at rest. Bind them at your wrist as a sign and let them be as a pendant on your forehead. Write them on the doorposts of your houses and on your gates. (Deut. 6:7–9)

The teaching of the Church and the words of Scripture should be laced into the daily events of our lives. This is one reason I enjoy the rhythm of the Church seasons: Advent, Christmas, Lent, Easter, Pentecost, and the rest. They regularly remind us of the great truths of the Christian life. Rather than criticize how materialism has infiltrated these celebrations, we ought to take them back and fill them with the presence of the Lord.

What the sacred Scripture is telling us is that we as Christian parents are supposed to be impressing the Word of God indelibly in the hearts, minds, and lives of our children. We have been given tremendous responsibility by the Lord and by the Church to stand as parents on behalf of the Lord, and to teach our children His truth.

We send our children to school to receive an education, but we can never confuse public education with truth. Intellectual truths about the world are important, but the truth of God is the greatest gift we can give our children. Public school often falls short in both of these critical areas of teaching, and so children do not receive the necessary truths of God in that environment. The tragedy that has beset our present era is that state laws actually forbid any kind of religious teaching or example. Gone are the days of prayer in the school and godly images on the walls of the classrooms. Moreover, there is often little to no example of dynamic Christian living in the classroom.

It is frequently difficult for children to learn even from the Church. We want them to see their membership in a church community as the number one means of support and evangelization. We want them to be excited about the ministry as a possible call for their lives. We want them to be totally surrendered and abandoned to God's power rather than their own. Unfortunately in my own tradition, the Catholic Church is currently experiencing a time of difficulty. But this is the case in many Christian churches. Membership is dropping, local churches are closing, and vocations to the ministry are decreasing—all warning signs of a generation that relies on self rather than God. These are not values that we want our children to accept.

Another danger within the Church is that specific teachings are often watered down or distorted in some sense. Even from the pulpit, our children are not often taught the radical truth of the Christian life. But aside from some dangerous teachings within the Church, a more fundamental problem exists. Church as a once or twice a week experience cannot be the primary source of education in the faith. Daily life in the domestic church is where they will receive the truth that sticks. My goal is not to be critical of the Church or our educational systems, but rather to be realistic about our responsibility as parents. If we want to change our nation and our Church, we must begin at home.

We want our children to be rooted in the truth, but this cannot happen fully anywhere but in the home. The every day experience of family life must be the primary source of education. They need to daily receive truth and begin in the home to daily live as members of the extended Christian family of the Church.

The process of ongoing instruction in Christian living is often called *catechesis,* from which we derive the word *catechism.* Pope John Paul II strongly encourages family catechesis:

"Family catechesis precedes, accompanies and enriches all other forms of catechesis. But above all it means that the family itself is the first and most appropriate place for teaching the truths of the faith, the practice of Christian virtues and the essential values of human life."[6]

It is hard work. It is hard work to be the parents the Lord really desires us to be, to be the educators of our children in faith. But anything good requires hard work, and we need to take this task seriously. We have the necessary grace to fulfill our parental role by virtue of the Sacrament of Marriage, a wellspring of grace upon which we can continually draw.

How to Do It

How can we devote ourselves to apostolic instruction? How can we make apostolic instruction available to our children? After all, most parents are not theologians or even teachers, and the thought of "instruction" may conjure up images of erecting a podium in the living room. But we are all aware that lectures do not strike the hearts of young children. Dr. James Dobson asserts that the key to family instruction is brevity.[7] We don't want our children to dread family prayer or instruction. Therefore, we must take into account their limited attention spans and their need for interesting teaching methods. Dry lectures rarely are effective for adults let alone youngsters. There are so many ways to instruct children so that they are interested and actually want to know more. We will explore some of these techniques later in the chapter.

We need to build in our homes a way of life that has apostolic instruction in it, regularly sharing the faith—sharing the faith around the dinner table, sharing the faith in morning and evening prayer, opening the sacred Scripture for our children, and giving them responsibility for reading, studying, and obeying the Bible and the teachings of the Church. We can, and we must, make our faith in Jesus Christ an ordinary part of our daily life. No one is perfect—especially me. God doesn't ask us to do it all perfectly. He knows what we are made of. He only asks for commitment and perseverance.

St. Jerome once said, "Ignorance of the Scripture is ignorance of Christ."[8] The Scripture is a blueprint for family life. There is much wisdom in it to help those of us who are called to family life. There are great chapters, such as Colossians 1 and Ephesians 5, that are marriage manuals filled with advice to husbands and wives, and to parents and children on how to love one another in the domestic church, and how to work out our salvation through the vehicle of the family.

We need to learn how to live those words with each other. Live the words of Christ? That means forgiveness should be a regular facet of our relationships. So many people have a difficult time saying "I'm sorry" because of pride or pain, but freedom begins with repentance and forgiveness. One of Jesus' main ministries was forgiveness of sin because He knew that was where people needed real healing.

Living the words of Christ also means love and sacrifice are actually our frame of reference not a biannual heroic deed.

We daily die to self and self's desires so that others might live.

Living the words of Christ means healing with compassion. When the child comes home from school crying because he feels stupid, inadequate, and left out, we are ready to salve the wound with genuine love, affirmation, and a tender embrace. Living the words of Christ means being ready for tears, anger, joy, and all other emotions; being ready to enter in to our families' affective experiences; and being ready to guide them in godly wisdom and truth, even when they rebel.

Obviously if we are to live these words, we must learn them first. We need to learn the sacred Scripture, the Word of God. If we really want to know who the Lord is, to know His ways and His mind, and if we really want to impart that to our children, we need to read, study, obey, and impart the teachings of the sacred Scripture regularly.

We can also help our children in practical ways. For those who are old enough to read, we encourage daily Bible reading. I and my wife try to show interest in their reading and prayer life. Of course, our plans don't always work out because of the hectic pace of our lives, but we try to set goals that we can meet realistically and adjust easily. We want to be assured that our children are reading the words of life and in relationship with their source, Jesus. This is how they will grow into the image of Jesus Christ and become all that God desires them to be.

Another great help to my family, as liturgical Christians, is the lectionary of the Church, which contains Bible readings that the whole Church hears proclaimed in the Liturgy of the Word every day at Mass.

We try to incorporate the daily readings of the liturgy into our family worship. This helps us remember as the domestic church our identity as a cell of the larger church. Every evening before dinner, when the children were younger, we used to have a family prayer time during which I or one of my children would read the gospel for that day. Then we would discuss and share it. My wife and I tried to instruct them in a way that they could understand, but we also invited their reflection on the readings. It is truly amazing how the Lord speaks to children. We have learned so much from our children and found this one of the most rewarding experiences of being parents.

We also find helpful teaching our children the traditions of our faith. As a Catholic Christian, sharing with our children about the role of the Mary, the mother of Jesus, is important. Her perfect yes to God continually reminds us of our need to be submissive and obedient to the Lord. In particular, the women in the family draw strength from the example of Mary. She is strong yet gentle, powerful yet obedient, and always in her motherly role showing the need for the feminine role in the Church.

In addition to specific verbal teaching, there is power in nonverbal tools that symbolize great truths of the faith. We try to fill our home with things that will remind us of where we are headed—heaven. The sacred Scripture says that we are aliens and pilgrims on this earth and we don't have here a lasting city (Heb. 13:14). We are, in fact, made for heaven. One of the greatest riches of being Christians is that we believe in an incarnational faith experience. So our primary symbol is the cross. Every time we look at the cross we are reminded of the love that God has for us. Therese of Liseux called prayer the bridge between heaven and earth. It is the most powerful symbol that shows us who we belong to and why.

We also try to have our home filled with Christian artwork that will instruct our families. One of the reasons for stained glass windows, originally, was to instruct the faithful in the mysteries of the faith. This was particularly important because many were illiterate. But it also acknowledged the need we have to see, feel, and touch the symbols of our faith. Humans (and especially children) have a great need to experience life through the five senses. For this reason, in our home we have religious art that we feel provides windows to heaven. When we see an icon we are reminded of the mysteries and heroes of the faith. Sometimes we think that icons and sacred things are supposed to be reserved for monasteries or convents, or religious houses, or perhaps some are afraid they detract from the centrality of God. But we have found that we can use them to instruct our children and turn our home into a domestic church.

Another thing we find helpful is books on the saints, the heroes of the faith. We try to use their lives as a vehicle for teaching our children what they should aspire to. The saints are the great cloud of witnesses the sacred Scripture talks about (Heb. 12:1), the heroes. Children respond to great Christians because they need and respond to heroes. In an age where there are antiheroes, people who stand for the opposite values of the kingdom, it is critically important that we hold up for our children true heroes, ones who went to their death for the cause of Christ, ones who gave up the things of this world for the sake of the kingdom. How much healthier and holier to have our son identify with Francis of Assisi or Martin Luther rather than Rambo, or our daughter pattern her life after Therese of Liseux or Susannah Wesley instead of Madonna. Give kids the gift of reading about the saints.

Many of the above ideas work well with my older children, but what about the young kids? Well, children love to read. Depending on their ages, they read different things. We're convinced that from their earliest age, we should fill their little minds with things about God. There are many children's books available to us such as *The Ten Commandments* and *The Eight Beatitudes*. They are written in such a way that they are interesting, and they make the children want to follow Jesus. In our age of VCRs, the opportunities are endless. Animated Bible stories on video, family entertainment—these are the things that kids can enjoy and learn from as well.

When properly used, the media can be an effective means of instruction. Actually, it can be a blessing or a curse. We must be painfully aware of what our children are receiving from the media. Proper instruction will help them from being seduced by the spirit of the age that is so prevalent in many current programs. I thank God for the Christian Broadcasting Network and the Eternal Word Television Network (a Catholic Christian network) with programs specifically for children and entire families as well. CBN's "Superbook" cartoon series is outstanding. The network also takes air time for prayer. My wife and daughters pray a special devotion called the Chaplet of Divine Mercy with the television broadcast on EWTN.

In addition to all these things, we also try to put into the daily pattern of our life events that support our Christian convictions. We have rediscovered a long-held treasure of the whole Christian church, the church year and the church calendar. We try to mark our time by great events of the faith. A couple of years ago we planted our first garden on the Feast of Isadore, the farmer considered to be the patron of gardens. That made an indelible mark on my son. It made him realize that God is interested in every aspect of our life, including growing vegetables.

These things are just our effort to take seriously the mandate the Lord gives us and the Church gives us, to teach our children the faith, to bring them up in apostolic instruction. All of these are specific tools for instruction in the faith, but as important as this phase is, our faith cannot be simply an intellectual construction.

Though many of these customs and traditions are clearly based upon my family's identity as Catholic Christians, the concepts are all transferrable, no matter what church community or tradition you belong to. Every church confession has men or women whose heroic love for God can become a model. Human beings all mark special times with special events, even the secular world. Let's sanctify our memories by remembering the wonderful mysteries of our faith.

My good friends Rob and Paul Schenck are Messianic Jewish Assemblies of God pastors. Over the years I have watched with great delight as their children have filled the year with Yom Kippur, Rosh Hashanah, Chanukah, Christmas, Easter, Pentecost . . . almost as if all of life were a celebration. That's the point! Christian family life should be the most exciting expression of life on earth. If it is, it will attract people to our God.

Again, for this reason, the most effective and lasting instruction for children is the witness of our lives, how our hearts are dedicated to the Lord. Through your witness, they should know what it means to love the Lord, to thirst for holiness, and to seek the kingdom. They have to be able to see your love for the Lord in ordinary day-to-day life.

We live in an age when love is bantered about as a term meaning all kinds of things. As believers, we understand love because we saw it demonstrated when Jesus Christ stretched out His arms on the cross. That's the kind of love we should be imparting to our children.

Love means I am willing to apologize when I hurt someone. Love means you desire the other's salvation above all else. Love means laying down your life for your family. Love means taking out the garbage when I'd rather lie on the couch. Love means giving my wife a listening ear when I'd rather shut myself off from the world at the end of a long day. For my wife, love means figuring out yet another way to prepare the chicken. Love is a big gift expressed in hundreds of little ways. This is what we should be teaching our children to do: *love,* love as Jesus loved.

Love cannot be caught by word alone. Did you ever sit in a classroom, hear a teaching, but then not live it? I know I have. This is sometimes what happens when we try to teach the faith to our children. Simply conveying it verbally is not sufficient.

Our teaching must be incarnational; we must weave it into our day-to-day experience of life. This is why parental teaching is a continual dynamic and is not finished until our children have acquired, owned, and begun to walk in what we have imparted to them.

Parents, we must teach our children the life-giving truths of our faith. Teaching is only one aspect of our responsibility. Hand in hand with teaching comes training. As Andrew Murray well defines it:

> Teaching is the communication of knowledge. . . . [Training] is the development of the faculties, both intellectual and moral, to help the child really to do and be what the teaching has set before him.[9]

We are responsible as cocreators with God to share with God the process of our children's development. We have a tremendous challenge to meet in the raising of children, and only by the grace of God can we guide our children so that one day on their own they will be able to choose the Lord. He is the Master Craftsman, but He uses our hands, hearts, and lives to train our children to act like Him. That's what we'll look at next.

8

Train Up A Child . . .

[Children are] immortal spirits whom God hath, for a time, entrusted to your care, that you may *train* them up in all holiness, and fit them for the enjoyment of God in eternity. This is a glorious and important trust, seeing one soul is of more value than all the world beside. Every child, therefore, you are to watch over with the utmost care, that when you are called to give an account of each to the Father of Spirits, you may give your accounts with joy and not with grief (emphasis added).[1]

John Wesley, in the above quote, put forth a solemn exhortation and a challenge for all Christian parents to train their children in the ways of God. But training involves more than doctrinal teaching or teaching our families right from wrong. Not even teaching through the example of our own lives is enough. There is an entirely separate dimension of raising children that involves actually a process of formation. The process involves building—building character, building virtue—growing in holiness.

Growing in holiness is a lifetime process, but as Christian parents, we have already had years of training (through family, church community, and/or personal prayer) and are now called to take up that same task with our children. Again, the first seven years of a child's life are critical for teaching and training. The concepts and habits they learn in these years (even if lost for a time) will come back at some point in their adult life. Train them early in the way of holiness. Train them to love God, to serve people, to persevere, to have courage and hope. Train them until these actions become habits. Habits of holiness formed in youth have a good chance of remaining throughout a child's life. Isn't this the goal?

The leaders of my church painted a very practical picture of how these holy habits are imparted:

> [Adolescent] training should be continued all through life, to fit them to meet the demands of fresh duties. . . . It rests with the parents to prepare their children from an early age, within the family circle, to discern God's love for all men; they will teach them little by little—and above all by their example—to have concern for their neighbor's needs, material and spiritual. The whole family, accordingly, in its community life should become a kind of apprenticeship to the apostolate.[2]

Isn't that marvelous? Did you ever think of that in terms of your training relationship with your children, Dad or Mom, that they are apprentices learning the life of holiness under your care. The term apprentice is not overly familiar in the twentieth-century mind, but the concept was a way of life just two hundred and even one hundred years ago. A son learned a trade from his father—perhaps a blacksmith, silversmith, or potter. Even Jesus Himself became a carpenter after years of tutelage under Joseph's care.

Today vestiges of the concept remain. We have employers train us for a new job, or we attend a workshop or seminar showing us how to be more efficient or more successful at any type of work. We know how to train for improved performance, but no longer do most people understand apprenticeship.

Apprenticeship

Training someone as an apprentice takes more. It takes commitment and a selfless, unconditional love. Franco Zefferelli in his production of *Jesus of Nazareth* sensitively portrays a beautiful scene between Joseph, Jesus, and other children. Joseph is teaching the children about carpentry, and at the same time intricately weaving into his instruction Jewish moral teaching. Joseph did not simply teach Jesus how to carve wood; he taught Jesus about life. He trained Jesus to live in a world that included more than just making a living.

As Christian parents, we've got to train our children for life. We are to be committed to the total person in our child, not just the mind or body or spirit. We need to do more than train our children to have good study habits or to prepare for a career. We need to do more than support our child's desire to be part of an athletic team. We need to do more than train our child with social graces so that he or she can relate well with others. We also need to do more than train our child to have a daily prayer time, to read the Bible, or to go to church. We need all of these elements for our child's healthy balance. We need to be committed to the growth of the whole person.

Most people readily agree with the above thoughts, but apprenticeship has another element of which many are unaware. This is the level of unconditional love, the teacher's selfless desire for the good of the student. A teacher trains with the goal of the apprentice's not only standing on his own two feet, but actually surpassing the ability of the teacher.

One of my favorite movies of all time is *Rocky III*. The entire series is wonderful, but the third installment is my favorite. If you have seen it, you may remember the role of Apollo Creed, Rocky's trainer. Apollo understood this dimension of training. In particular, I remember the scene where Apollo was training Rocky in speed and endurance. Together every day they ran on the beach, energized by the rush of the crashing waves. Apollo always pulled ahead, eventually beat Rocky, and then proceeded to encourage and challenge him.

Finally one magic day on the beach, it happened. Every moment of training led to this point. Rocky, with sheer determination and every ounce of strength, finally outran Apollo. The disciple had outrun the master. The scene is a culmination of events, symbolic of the new level of physical and emotional endurance that Rocky has reached. The interesting thing, however, is Apollo's reaction. He was not angry or disappointed or bitter or jealous. He understood the goal and so he rejoiced with his friend, hugging, jumping, laughing. Apollo understood training and so must we.

A similar relationship exists in the Jewish tradition: that of a rabbi and his student. The rabbi teaches and helps to form the mind and heart of his student. He also hopes that his student excels beyond what he can teach.

These relationships are centered on *other* not *self.* The teacher always seeks the greatest good for the student. The Christian family is no different. In fact, we need to become the models for that kind of training. We parents have naturally received the role of teacher for our children. Like Apollo Creed, and like the rabbi, we should rejoice as they come closer to the crown of life. We rejoice as they attain the goal set before them.

Goal: Becoming Like Jesus

But we must have God's goal for our family in mind. God's goal is that our children become more like Christ even though our goals for our children might be different. We may want them to be and do everything that we could not, but we harm our children when we try to live out our agenda through them. We harm our children when we fix their eyes on false and empty goals. We can harm our children when we beat it into their heads that they are going to be the best lawyer, doctor, accountant, or even Christian leader if the source of our prodding is our own desire to live our unfulfilled goals through them.

What happens if the career we choose for a child is not the call that God has for his life? What happens when the desire of the child's heart is vastly different from the parent's desire? Inevitably the child will either carry unhealthy guilt or be trapped in a job that he does not want. Obviously neither of these things will allow the fullness of life and joy God wants for our children.

The goal is *not* success or comfort in the world's eyes, but faithfulness in God's eyes. We train our children for life, eternal life. We ought to train them in sanctification and evangelization—growing in holiness and sharing God's life.

The goal of our training should be to present our children to God as faithful disciples. Faithfulness is, after all, the most critical attribute of a follower of Christ. My friend Chuck Colson has a wooden paperweight prominently displayed in his office. It bears the inscription "Faithfulness, not success." He says the saying comes from Mother Teresa of Calcutta. She once told a reporter, "I do not find the word *success* in the Bible, only *faithfulness.*" In an age of success-orientation and misguided "prosperity theology," we need to turn our children to Jesus, not careers.

We know that our task is training the kids to form habits of holiness, following the way of the cross, but it seems an overwhelming task doesn't it? Training is hard work both for trainer and trainee. Anyone who has trained hard for something knows the time, repetition, practice, and dedication that is necessary to be serious about attaining a goal. It is admirable and noble to reach for a goal. We admire the Olympic decathlete who labors and fine tunes his every movement to be able to compete in the games. We admire the Russian gymnasts who begin training even as their bones are still in the formative process. It takes years, and we admire them.

How much more should we admire the Christian who has built character by standing firm in the times of persecution! The Christian who has set her eyes on the cross and never looked away. The Christian who chases after the crown of glory. These are the goals that we lay before our children, and these are the principles in which we form them.

How to Train Them in Spiritual Disciplines

Religious training is possible for our children; it is not just something that happens to men and women training for a life of ministry. I have attempted in this book to chop away the false wall that people build between the religious and the human, the spiritual and the secular. Religious training is movement toward holiness, a holiness of daily living to which *all* are called.

There are so many ways to train our children in holiness. To begin with, we can help them grasp the foundation of their faith by learning, memorizing, and repeating the many form prayers at our disposal. Many people scoff at form prayers, but I find them tremendously helpful for my own prayer life, to establish rhythm, meditation, and contemplation. Many times I have difficulty entering into prayer until I meditate on the great mysteries of our faith while praying a series of prayers in a private devotion. Or I might concentrate on the love of my heavenly Father and His plan for my life as I pray the "Our Father." Or I might recommit myself to God as a baptized Christian as I pray the "Apostle's Creed."

All of these prayers grew out of a need in the early church. Form prayers grew out of a learned experience of a Christian people who had their hearts in the *parousia,* but not seeing it happen, set their sights on the long haul. They began to teach their families the faith through prayers. When others came to join the church, they too were taught the faith. They were (and still are today) called *catechumens.* They were catechized, trained in the faith. Part of their training before baptism was rote repetition of prayers. A similar principle is engaged today when we memorize Scripture. We want the faith to be on our minds, lips, and hearts, to be rooted deep in our spirits.

Form prayers have often been helpful for my family. I remember one day after a lengthy, draining discussion on morality and behavior and authority, my wife, two oldest kids, and I decided we should pray. Nobody was able to muster the energy or desire for spontaneous prayer. None of us really knew what to pray. So instead, we said an "Our Father," a "Hail Mary," and a "Glory Be" to allow God to work in our hearts. Interestingly after these prayers, we all felt led to ask for forgiveness and strength for our particular weaknesses. The form prayer released us from the emotional feelings of anger and hurt, and we were led into the intimate presence of God. It won't always work that way. Prayer is often devoid of feeling, but our children need to learn to pray *especially* when they don't feel like it. They need to learn to focus on God at all times, to tap into His presence with every available means. So do we.

Regarding prayer, our children should also learn to be responsible for a daily time of prayer, differing according to age. As parents, it is important to be flexible with our children here. Our role is to facilitate growth and habitual action in this area, not dread or guilt. Our children need to know the joy and fruit of prayer, and how prayer gives us a steadfastness, a rootedness, and a peace. We cannot wait until we "have it all together" before we teach them. Not only does that breed false guilt, legalism, and insecure parenting, but it means most of us would never teach our children about daily prayer because very few adults "have it all together."

Discipline

Formation, however, is more than training our children in spiritual disciplines. Another growth is the ability to see discipline as a structured form of love and rejoice in it. The word *discipline* is taken from the same root as *disciple*. Discipling our children involves discipline. No teaching will be effective for a child if there are no consequences for disobedience to the teaching.

Children will never learn right if we reinforce their wrong. Wrong must be corrected with proper discipline. Tough love has got to be one of the hardest things for a parent to maintain. Sometimes when I know I need to discipline one of my kids, and I look at the quivering lips and eyes welling up with tears, I feel I'll never have the strength to correct him or her. My emotional love can get in the way of agape love, the greater love. We know there are times when firm correction is more loving than a pat on the back and a "try harder next time, honey." The Scriptures show us that God disciplines those whom He loves. The author of Hebrews tells us that if He does not discipline us, we are not sons (Heb. 12:8).

A parent's relationship with his or her child should be modeled after God's relationship with humans, a love relationship of gentleness and mercy.

> As God's love for us leads him to gently correct our sinful ways, so a parent's love leads a father to guide, correct, and even bring some pain to the child when it is necessary for his eventual good.[3]

The Scripture reads: "For the moment all discipline seems painful rather than pleasant; later it yields the peaceful fruit of righteousness to those who have been trained by it (Heb. 12:11 RSV).

So discipline is necessary, but only healthy if administered in the proper way. Many parents, in the name of discipline, verbally or even physically abuse their children. Instead of a parent's unconditional love in action, "discipline" becomes an unhealthy outlet for anger, frustration, a need for control, or any other latent issue. Not only is this an unhealthy means of working out emotions, but it is also a dangerous inroad for our child to potentially take on similar patterns.

On the other hand, a lack of discipline in the home (some would call this permissiveness), is equally dangerous. This structure sets up the child as coequal to parent in terms of authority. Certainly a child's dignity as a person and right to be respected is equal, but equal authority between parent and child will most likely not peacefully coexist. Parents cannot allow the child to choose his bedtime, what chores he will and will not do, or how she will treat other members of the family. What danger we open our children up to when we grant their every desire! How will they ever learn the Christian virtues of sacrifice, obedience, and selflessness if never learned in youth?

By learning to yield to the loving guidance of his parents, a child learns to submit to other forms of authority that will confront him later in life—teachers, employers, leaders of the church. Most importantly, respect of earthly authority helps a child later respond to the holy promptings of his God. This fruit is the goal of parental training. Controlling our children is not our desire. In fact, the best guidance helps our children become more independent of the parent and increasingly dependent on God. That's what true discipleship is all about, helping the disciple to become fully mature and able to make decisions rooted in a formed conscience.

What is Proper Discipline?

How can children be disciplined in a way that will help them to grow without becoming resentful? I believe, and James Dobson agrees, that parents should begin teaching a child about discipline and self-control by external influences.

> By being required to behave responsibly, he gains valuable experience in controlling his own impulses and resources. Then as he grows into the teen years, the transfer of responsibility is made year by year from the shoulders of the parent directly to the child.[4]

In the early years, external discipline is useful. At times, even physical discipline is appropriate. For instance, when a small child finds a fascinating set of holes in the wall and wants to do more exploring, then a quick spank is better than allowing him to make his own decision. Rationalizing and reasoning with a crawling, curious one year old will not do the trick. Physical discipline, however, can never be the only vehicle. It works hand in hand with certain forms of deprivation and verbal discipline.

By deprivation I do not mean withholding anything essential for a child's healthy body, mind, or spirit. But by way of discipline, it can be effective to deprive a child, for a period of time, of certain privileges such as television or free time with friends. Have the child fill that time with more chores around the house or more homework. Never deprive your child, however, of love and affection, support and encouragement.

With regard to verbal discipline, I believe there are two ex-

121

tremes, and both are equally dangerous. The first is verbal abuse, and it can take many forms. One common form is yelling at our children without listening to an explanation. Often this is our way of taking the anger or frustration from our day and projecting it onto the kids. How many times have we all done that? I certainly do it more often than I would like to admit.

Assaulting our children with words or a tone of voice can leave them with permanent scars. As assistant prosecuting attorney in Ohio, I worked for the state's juvenile department. The stories that I have heard from many of the kids broke my heart. Physical, verbal, mental, emotional, and sexual abuse are rampant, but verbal abuse is among the most damaging. Many kids suffer from such a lack of self-worth and low self-esteem because they have been fed lies about how stupid, lazy, worthless, or selfish they are. We need to correct the old maxim, "Sticks and stones will break my bones, but names will never hurt me." It's not true! Any type of condemnation, whether it comes in the form of name-calling or belittling, is detrimental to a child, especially one whose identity is in the formative stages. The internal wounds of these experiences are often irreparable.

The opposite extreme to verbal abuse is a lack of any verbal discipline. This type of parent fears being overly harsh with the child and damaging her emotions. Again, this is a very real concern, and so we should always take the utmost care in the way we speak with our children.

Jesus, of course, models the perfect balance between verbal abuse and firm correction, even though He is more stern at times than others. For instance, in the garden of Gethsemane, Jesus reproves Peter, James, and John for failing to remain awake and on guard while He prayed. The disciples were in training, and Jesus showed them the danger of becoming lukewarm. He said in essence, "Wake up, be alert. You never know the hour of temptation or death. Always be on guard so you won't fall from relationship with Me." He disciplined the three for their failure to stay alert. His reproof, as always, was for their good, given as a warning for future temptations.

Jesus also became more harsh when circumstances dictated. For example, Peter was abruptly corrected once by Jesus, even though his motives were pure. Peter, rock of the Church. Peter, first to confess Jesus as Messiah. Peter, present at all the major events in the gospel. Peter. We often expect Peter, as the man chosen by God to lead the Church, to be smoothly polished rock—no cracks, no flaws, not even any dents. But Peter was as human as you and I, and he had a great love for the Lord Jesus. Because of his love for Jesus, his heart was broken as he heard of the future of his Friend and Master—death on a cross. Probably in emotional turmoil, Peter approached Jesus with his concern.

Now Jesus knew where Peter's heart was, yet He still corrected him. He said, "Get behind me Satan." In other words, "Do not tempt Me away from the plan, you adversary" (*Satan* means "adversary"). Peter's human desires and fears forced him out of relationship as advocate, and he became adversary.

Jesus used verbal discipline, verbal correction. He used it with the disciples, with the Pharisees, and with the crowds. He gave us a model of correction within our structure of formation. Discipline is one important key to proper, healthy, balanced formation of our children.

Affirmation

Always with discipline comes an incredible need for affirmation. One of the most profound and tragic realities the family faces is an overall lack of secure identity. Children are starved for affirmation and affection, and it is within the natural bond of family that affirmation takes place.

As I have already expressed, there has been a breakdown in the extended family where the nuclear family is the sole source of life. In earlier times, the whole extended family was responsible for supporting and encouraging one another. Mom, Dad, kids, grandparents, aunts, uncles, cousins together became a living pool of affirmation to the child. Now in this nuclear family, the heavy responsibility of affirming and unconditionally loving the children falls on the shoulders of Mom and Dad alone. This is not the way it was meant to be. That's why it doesn't work! To allow children the fullest experience of support is the best way to ensure that their needs of affirmation are met. By God's grace we have begun to see our own extended family begin to reunite. We have also begun to see just how important the Body of Christ is in providing an environment of support for the family.

Training the Will

All of these techniques—apprenticeship, discipline, affirmation—help parents order the minds and hearts of their children to God. The children, in turn, have a firm foundation from which to make the proper choices in life. As parents, we teach our children how to choose. That's completely different from making choices for them. Each of our children, as you and I, has been endowed with the most awesome gift of free will that they must exercise in order to be fully human. We want to avoid dehumanizing our children by controlling them. Rather, we want to help stir within them the desire to *choose* serving the family, going to church, praying on their own. And we want them to form habits of choosing the good.

Andrew Murray provides some clear insight into the difficulty of combining this freedom with a healthy obedience.

God's Word more than once taught that obedience is the child's first virtue—that in yielding to it his will is to be exercised. He is to obey not because he understands or approves, but because the parent commands. In this he will become the master of his own will as he voluntarily submits it to a higher authority. Obedience from this principle will thus secure a double good: while guiding the will into right habits, it strengthens the command the child has over it. When this has been attained, a safe foundation has been laid for the further exercise of the child's free will in the deliberate choice of what appears to him best. It is this that the parent must regard as his highest and most blessed work . . . it is the parent's influence that must train the young will to exercise the power on which, in later life, everything depends; he must now be trained himself to refuse the evil and choose the good. . . . Dear parents, God's highest gift to man in creation was the will, that he might choose the will of his God. Your highest work is to take charge of that will in your child and be God's minister in leading it back to His service.[5]

Murray confirms that our number one priority as parents is training our children. The Scriptures tell us to "Train up a child in the way he should go, and when he is old he will not depart from it" (Prov. 22:6 RSV). The Word speaks to our responsibility for every soul we bring into this world. They are under our care for a season, and the way we tend to them in those few early years affects the rest of their lives on earth and possibly their eternal salvation.

Look How They Love

As seriously as I take the Word of God, my scriptural charge to train my children is not the only thing that motivates me. I love my children with a father's love, and I care for their future. But I also have a profound respect for my kids. I realized some time ago that God respects my children. He respects their free will, their dignity, and their ability to receive love and care from others. Often I have marveled at the capacity of children to love, to be in awe, to wonder and delight. They can look at the same exact scene or hear the same story that I do, yet they inevitably see and hear things I do not.

Socrates believed that children are born with all wisdom, but increasingly forget that wisdom as they age. For him, the role of teaching is to bring back that wisdom, in a sense, to draw out what a person already knows. As Christians we can use Socrates's notion and explain wisdom as the capacity to love. Children are endowed with a great capacity to love and thus great wisdom. But the world drains them of it. I believe the role of the Christian parent then is to protect and enhance the child's capacity to love.

Respecting and working with our children's God-given gifts is really the heart of training. Instead of only following the commands of God, we follow the Spirit speaking truth about our children deep in our hearts. The depth and responsibility of the call of Christian parents must resound deeply within if we are to find the strength to combat all the potential difficulties that may stand in the way of our children's training in the holy ways of God.

9

Incarnational Power and Thanksgiving

We have established that the family is clearly a miniature model of the Church at large, and in its communal dimension is found the power to live the call of the Church. The Body of Christ is a completely communal reality. From the moment of baptism, the incorporation into the Body of Christ, we surrender self to the community of the Church. As members of that community, we should understand that everything we do affects the entire Body of Christ.

Our actions are significant—sin, virtue, prayer, even the manifestation of our emotions in joy, sorrow, or love, in some way affect the Body of Christ. There can be no "private" moments after we become intimately linked to Christ and His Body. We do have "personal" moments flowing from a person-to-person relationship with Jesus, but nothing is private or "just between me and God."

We need to see both dimensions of relationship, personally to Christ and communally with His Body, as the means to salvation. God in His infinite generosity has left us the perfect channels to express and share our relationships and to live out our call as the Church. To do this, He has provided for us the grace of the sacramental life. So many times the gift of the sacraments, the gift of Jesus Himself, is abused, misunderstood, or reduced to a mindless ritual.

Many of you do not belong to sacramental Christian churches and may not understand my perspective on the sacraments. In my understanding, God reveals Himself to us through the sacraments. They are a picture of His love for us. God has expressed His love perfectly through His perfect Son, Jesus. In that way Jesus is *the* "Sacrament" of the Father. "He is the image of the invisible God" (Col. 1:15). And God still expresses His love in very physical ways. Nature is sacramental because it reveals the glory and love of God (Rom. 1). The Church itself is sacramental in that it reflects the love and ministry of Christ. In my church marriage is a sacrament, a reflection of the mystery of Christ and His church. My whole spirituality is sacramental, or incarnational. If you are a Christian, so is yours. I respect the various views of the sacraments within the Christian church, and I would not try to change your position. So, although your tradition may differ from mine somewhat, please read this chapter in light of the Incarnation and try to apply its principles to your own church experience.

As the Church, we need to recapture the power available in the sacraments and begin to tap into this reality. Only then can we function on the intimate, loving, relational level that we are called to by our Creator. The process, however, does not begin on a worldwide scale. But if we as the domestic church experience the risen Savior in the sacramental life, we can (as one unit in an extended community) affect the entire life of the Church.

As Father Michael Scanlan asserts in *And Their Eyes Were Opened,* the sacraments will not come alive until The Sacrament, the Church, is alive.[1] How can we expect vitality in the sacramental life unless the body of believers is alive and hungry? Are our families voraciously seeking the Lord? Are they seeking Him in a personal way? Are we taking seriously and rejoicing in our call as domestic church?

Answers to these questions require prayerful attentiveness to our personal and familial relationship to the Lord. If we are going to be the living, dynamic church on mission, we need to first know our motivation and then use the tools given to accomplish our goals. Jesus Christ must be the living, breathing inspiration for our lives, the primary person toward whom all of our lives point. But Christ Himself is at the same time the instrument of our salvation. He is the means and the end, the first and the last.

If Jesus is the locus for our spiritual growth, we should desire to become more attuned to His reality in our lives. It is so easy and natural to foster a distant relationship to God. After all, He is Creator, King, Lord, Savior, Master, God. He is truly awesome and deserves more honor, glory, worship, and adoration than we can ever muster or even imagine.

The mystery remains, however, that although transcendent in His glory, He is still somehow immanent in our now moment. Our God is close, and He has revealed to us that He is a God of relationships. He has created us to live in a covenant, committed relationship with Him. How do we know this? Because God chose to reveal Himself in the person of Jesus Christ. He did not have to use the vehicle of humanity, but He did. The emphasis on personhood and relationships in the Gospels is astounding. Throughout Scripture we see Jesus moving among the people, loving and caring for them as persons. What does this say for us if we are to follow the example of Christ? It says that we are to be people of relationships, first and foremost concerned with our one-on-one relationship with Christ, and second with all He has claimed as His own.

Like any other friendship, we need to meet Jesus frequently in order to grow. But we also need to have moments with Him that are not only special memories, but also points of real growth together, times where we reach a profoundly new level of relationship. These are the "sacramental" moments in our lives. These are the deeply personal encounters with God. Sacraments are best understood as Jesus reaching out to us, now saving, now forgiving, now uniting, now empowering, now healing, now touching us and calling us into deeper relationship with Him.[2] Jesus and me in the now moment within the Church family.

We must always be sensitive to the delicate balance between the personal encounter with Christ and the communal dimension of the Church and the sacraments. I believe that Christ chose the Church as a vehicle of grace in these special moments of our lives. There would be no sacraments without the Church, and so we must see the important role of the entire Body within each personal, sacramental moment. In particular, our families have a special role for each other in the sacramental life because the family is the immediate community and source of support for the faithful.

The community at large and the community of the family are important aspects of each of the seven sacraments of the Church. However, the domestic church plays a particularly vital role in the Sacraments of Reconciliation, Eucharist, and Marriage.

Restoring Harmony

The rite of reconciliation (also called confession) has, since the Second Vatican Council, changed its emphasis from penance for the actual sin to a reconciliation of relationships that have been damaged by sin. The new rite seeks to heal the relationship between the penitent and God, as well as the community. Here is where a proper understanding of a personal relationship with God is necessary. If one does not know the Lord as Friend and Brother and does not have a living relationship with Him, he will not understand the need to reconcile. Many fulfill the obligation to confess their sins, but have no concept of restoring a relationship with the Lord or with the Body of Christ. There is often no relationship to restore because there is no personal relationship with Jesus nor a sense of belonging to God's family.

As parents, we should teach our children to embrace Jesus as Friend and Confidant, even more personal than their human friends and family. We should teach them that when they sin, they hurt God just as they can hurt a neighborhood friend or schoolmate. This is what it means to instill in our children a holy fear of the Lord. We should not teach them to fear being in His presence or to constantly fear His wrath, but rather to fear breaking His heart. If our children mature continually growing in relationship with Christ, continually falling more and more in love with Him, they will eventually understand the pain that is involved in sin, both for God and ourselves. When we truly love, we would rather do anything than hurt our beloved.

Unfortunately because of our fallen nature, we do sin and we do offend the Lord. But in His tender compassion, He has provided a way to be forgiven. We need to be forgiven, to be reconciled if the relationship is to grow. That is why I have such an appreciation for the Sacrament of Reconciliation wherein I acknowledge my sin, ask forgiveness for the offense against God, and am absolved by God through the power He has given the Church.

Many of us realize the need to right our relationship with God, but do not see our need for the role of a priest or minister. A fuller understanding of community, however, reveals the damage sin causes the community. Sin not only wounds our relationship with God, but it also damages our relationship with the entire body. Remember what we established earlier! Everything we do affects the body in some way; there are no "private" sins. Every sin we commit wounds the entire body. So we need to be reconciled to God and also to His body, and therefore, the minister not only stands in the place of Christ, but also in the place of the community. Again, as a Catholic Christian, I believe that those ordained as church leaders have been given the authority, through Christ's death and resurrection, to forgive sins in His name. The apostle John, an eyewitness to the resurrection recounts in his Gospel that Jesus appeared to His disciples saying:

"Peace be with you. As the Father has sent me, so I send you."
And when he had said this, he breathed on them and said to them,
"Receive the holy Spirit. Whose sins you forgive are forgiven
them, and whose sins you retain are retained." (John 20:21–23)

But all Christians understand the corporate dimension of sin and forgiveness, even if they do not agree on the role of the

Church and her ministers in the process. The letter of James reminds us:

> Therefore confess your sins to each other and pray for each other so that you may be healed. (James 5:16 NIV)

If a person has no real sense of being part of a community, he will most likely not respond to full reconciliation within the Church family. As parents, we need to raise our children with that sense of community within the family. Our families need to become responsible to one another for their actions. Often in addition to sacramental confession, this means reconciling with each other face to face.

We all know how difficult it is to say we are wrong, especially to a brother or sister, but this is so important in the family. It requires true humility and death to self.

We have tried to instill this sense of responsibility for the consequences of sin in our children, as well as the need for repentance and reconciliation. Whenever they hurt one another, and we are aware of it, we call them to seek forgiveness. Contrary to what some contemporary thinkers would say, this has not riddled our children with guilt—precisely the opposite! It has brought them true freedom. At the other side of confession is forgiveness and healing.

These are the virtues that help our families grow in love and trust for one another. These are the fruits of forgiveness, the fruits of an encounter with Christ. Through the sacrament, we receive more grace to be healed and transformed, to avoid sin and to seek this full reconciliation with the Lord and His body daily.

The Body and Blood

When we are reconciled to God and the Church, we can then enter into the communal celebration of the Eucharist, "the source and summit of the Christian life."[3] Together the community primarily offers Christ the Lamb—and in a secondary sense, themselves—to the Father as they take part in the timeless event of Calvary. We each play a part in the action, and so unity of mind and heart is critical here. When one member of the body fails to enter fully into the sacrament, the body does not achieve the potential unity offered by Christ.

This is why there is disarray and disunity in the Church. We need to realize the potential impact of the Eucharist. Christ Himself is actually present, body and blood, soul and divinity, and He Himself invites us to become living, walking, breathing tabernacles. He invites us to become His dwelling place and be transformed by His loving presence! The deepest reality of the sacrament is true communion, intimate union with God and His body, the Church. This is what God offers us, but whether this happens or not depends on how each individual responds to the grace of God's gift of self.

The greatest, most loving act we can do for our children is to teach them reverence, respect, and excitement for the sacrament of the altar. Some time ago, my then eight-year-old son Keith made the mistake of thinking he was going to receive his First Communion in first grade. He really looked forward to it, but one day his teacher told the class that they would not receive communion until the second grade. He came home from school feeling rather disturbed and shared with me his disappointment. I tried to encourage him by saying, "Keith, it won't be long. Another few months and you will receive it." But I realized as I listened to him how much he was longing for the Eucharist, and I thanked God for his desire. That desire still has not changed.

Our families should become eucharistic, constantly aware of the dynamic, healing presence of Christ in our midst. He has made Himself available in the most intimate ways for us so that we can experience Christ in the sacraments as the center of our faith. To me, nothing is as powerful as the experience of receiving the body and blood of the Lord in His Holy Supper.

Receiving the Lord's Supper, the Eucharist, is a sense experience of the Lord. The Church has long held that the only way we can come to knowledge of about any given thing is to first receive data through the senses. The intellect can only work if it has data to process. That data comes through our senses. God knew that because He created us that way and He sent His Son in the flesh. And it remains so—Jesus with us in the flesh in a mysterious way.

I believe the Eucharist is the only sacrament where we actually receive the Lord into our own flesh and blood. It stands to reason then, that the more often I receive the Lord, the more He will become part of me. For me, frequent reception of the Eucharist is transforming. We want our families to be transformed more and more into a reflection of Christ's Body on earth, the domestic church, and each individual member to be transformed into an *alter Christus,* "other Christ," an image of Jesus to the world.

All we have said up to now—the calling of the Holy Spirit, the teaching, training, praying—all of these are important, but I believe that the sacraments are a critical part of the process. They are a free gift of God's power breaking into our lives and transforming them. I don't know about you, but I need all of His power I can get in this vocation of family life!

We should be instilling in our children a love and a hunger for the Eucharist because it is their sustenance. Teach them about the beauty of Christ's loving sacrifice as a gift but also as an example of the need for sacrifice in the home. Teach them that the Eucharist is like a huge reservoir of power just waiting to be tapped. Show them by example the change that can take place through the grace of the Eucharist. Show them the actualization of communion, of unity in the home. Allow the sacrament to change your family into a true brotherhood and sisterhood, united under the banner of Christ.

We try to partake in the sacrament often as a family. We can teach our children in those moments after receiving the Lord's Supper that the power of Jesus just made us more "one" as a family, more united. It would be great if every family could get to a daily communion service together. The power of that action would be explosive. But that's not very realistic, is it? With work and school and various activities, it is difficult enough to get an evening meal together, let alone a morning or midday service.

Besides, not every church tradition offers such frequent celebrations of the Lord's Supper.

But we can use our time together as a family to foster such a "eucharistic attitude" even if we can't get to a communion service. Such an attitude would focus primarily on the action of our family's seeking deep union with God and communion with each other. The family meal provides a perfect opportunity for parents to remind the children of this. Every meal holds incredible symbolism that we should highlight for our children. We can all learn to capitalize more fully on the language of symbol. Symbols speak loudly and clearly.

Tom Howard, in *Hallowed Be This House,* posits a meal as a ritual act of exchange. He says that whenever we sit down to eat,

> We are receiving life by chewing and swallowing the life of
> something else. . . . This food is really exchanged life; but it is
> only in the eucharistic vision that this becomes apparent. . . . Life
> laid down so that other life may spring forth. Life from death. . . .
> The sitting down around this table with our family is an act in
> which we . . . enact our common indebtedness to the order of
> exchanged life. . . . For Christians, of course, the whole thing is
> caught up in the biggest transaction of all, namely, the life of the
> Lamb of God laid down so that we might live.[4]

Show the family the sanctity of sitting at the table together, breaking bread, sharing our lives, teaching one another, growing in relationship, growing in love. These experiences prepare us for times when we will be called to lay down our lives for one another. That sacrifice is the greatest eucharistic fruit for the family. This is cause for true thanksgiving.

The evening meal as a family can be a symbol and reality of the communal dimension of family. But just as important, we should nurture in our children a personal sense of the eucharistic presence of the Lord. As important and primary as is Eucharist within the context of a formal church liturgy, there are other ways to experience an intimate communion. I have tried to open my children up to the experience of "spiritual communion," a Catholic Christian tradition I learned as a child.

Spiritual communion involves a few moments of silence at a given moment in the day to surrender self completely to the presence of God and seek deep communion, a "being with," a healing presence. Remaining close with God, uniting our spirit with His throughout the day helps us to walk in the light, to make clear choices, to love more deeply. We experience the treasure of faith kept alive in the heart, spirit, and home.

What God Has Joined Together

Eucharist and reconciliation, communion and forgiveness— these are the foundation stones for the building of any community, including the family. But we begin to build our family lives specifically on the grace found in the Sacrament of Marriage. This entire book is a fruit of meditation on the holy call of matrimony. With the high rate of divorce and dysfunctional families within the Church, it is fair to say that many couples have not responded to the grace that this sacrament offers. For Christians who view marriage as an ordinance, the power of the Lord breaks forth through the covenant they make before God and His people.

A large part of the problem is that we often do not provide communal support for the marriage or the family, nor do the partners understand their responsibility to the broader Church community. Marriage has become an exclusive event between two people who carry on their lives apart from the community. All of the couple's attention is focused on each other, and later on the children. What happens to the mission of the domestic church if we stay within the confines of our own family? There is no fulfillment of mission if outreach grinds to a halt at the marriage altar.

Additionally, without the support of the Christian community, the entire responsibility for the marriage falls on the couple alone. What an awesome responsibility! Christianity is by nature a social experience. We are committed to the Lord and to the community of faith. We need to share times of need and times of joy. We should pray together and play together and inspire one another. We should love one another as a body.

The nature and purpose of marriage clearly reveal the importance of involving others in our commitment. Marriage in a way represents the New Covenant, the bond that Christ established with the Church. This bond is relational, creative, intimate—all of the things that we as the Church experience in relationship with Christ. That's why we can call marriage "the Church in miniature."

In the marriage ceremony, the faith community is symbolically represented by the witnesses, best man and maid of honor, and the priest or minister. The witnessing, however, is in God's eyes actually done by the couple. Each witnesses the marriage for the other. The spouse is the agent of grace for the other, and so each becomes a minister of the sacrament. After all, the covenant is between them and God. Even though the couple administers the sacrament to themselves, the community should be present because the ceremony is more completely represented in the context of the ritual. The important thing to remember is that the *union* of the two people, not the wedding ceremony, is the sacrament, filled with God's grace and power.

Two persons desiring to unite with each other and God beautifully express agape love, pointing each other to the deepest reality and truth of existence: full union with God. Through this form of trinitarian love (two persons plus God), each partner attempts to lead the other to a fuller experience of salvation, and God constantly provides His presence and grace. Husbands and wives, we need to understand our role as channel and vessel of grace for our partner. We have chosen to be a means through whom our spouse works out his or her salvation. This commitment requires tremendous self-sacrifice and service to both the spouse and God. It means not using or manipulating each other to get needs or desires met. It means constantly dying to self and seeking the greatest love for the other. It's a tall order and a true vocation to discipleship.

This sounds like an incredible task, and it is. It is a supernatural task with needs that can only supernatural means can fulfill. Once again, God realized our needs and provided for us. We receive grace in the sacrament that empowers us to fulfill our call as marriage partners and parents. But the grace from the sacrament is not just a one-shot deal on the day of the wedding. No, Christ has established it as an enduring fountain of grace that we must daily draw from in our task as the domestic church. What a blessing to be daily renewed, strengthened, and guided by the ongoing grace of the Sacrament of Marriage. We simply need to call upon God, who was there in the covenant.

We can draw upon this strength every day in prayer as we ask the Lord to reign in our marriages, to rule in our homes, and to guide us as families to holiness. When our marriages are in order, our entire families have a greater chance to blossom under Gods power and guidance. We need to show our children from an early age the responsibility and commitment involved in marriage, but also the joy and satisfaction that is part of this holy calling.

In all of the sacraments, we need to see Jesus on a personal mission for each one of us, desiring to bring us into the fullest relationship possible with Him. The sacraments provide for us a channel of grace, an avenue toward full Christian living. We can meet Jesus in the sacraments in a way that nothing else can provide. The beauty of this is that Jesus set up the system. He wants us to encounter Him on this level. He wants intimacy. He wants commitment. He wants unity. He wants renewal.

Let us in our homes renew our fervor for the personal gifts that Jesus has given us. God will honor our efforts in our own lives and bless the Church through us.

Give Thanks with a Grateful Heart

There is another whole dimension of living sacramentally than responding to grace and acting in its power. We should always be aware of being grateful to the Lord for the blessings of life. We have been called to be family in the heart of the Church, and we have been given the power to live out this call. If we see family as the gift that it is, our response should be one of thanksgiving. We are actually able to share in the creative power of God, to be responsible for the hearts and souls of our children, and to live a life of love united in body and spirit with our spouse. What an incredible gift married life is!

In our homes, we can and should instruct our children to live out the call to be a thankful people, a people who are happy because they are called into relationship with God, a people who are happy to be family and appreciate the gifts of God. Thanksgiving should be the hallmark of our family life. For this to be so, we need to understand what thanksgiving is all about from a biblical perspective.

The Psalms are full of prayers of thanksgiving. That is why it is a good thing to pray the Psalms in family worship. Sometimes we try to use the Psalms around the dinner table, to imbibe David's spirit of thanksgiving. In Psalm 35 he cried out, "I will give you thanks, O Lord, in the vast assembly!" And in Psalm 52, he prayed, "I will thank you always for what you have done, and proclaim the goodness of your name." This type of thanksgiving (even when you don't feel like it) can really lift a drooping spirit.

People of the Old Testament understood that they had an obligation to give thanks to God. They called an assembly first to do that. And at various times in their history, they recalled what God had done for them as a people. They gathered as families to recount God's action on their behalf. Well, every family has a history of God's action on their behalf if they only pause to remember it. We can institute continual reminders, remembrances of God's blessings to our family. We try to weave these celebrations into the natural events of family life, for instance, on each child's birthday.

It helps to build a family history that centers around God's saving action for our family. We ought to recall the times when the Lord rescued us from financial difficulties or from health struggles. In times together around the dinner table or special times of celebration, we should call to mind the specific blessings of God.

One celebration that I have always been fond of is found in the

Old Testament book of Nehemiah. It is a celebration of thanksgiving for the rebuilding of the walls of Jerusalem. The Jews took the return of thanksgiving to God so seriously that they assigned whole families to various tasks, such as singing, ministry, playing instruments (Neh. 12). What a festivity!

The New Testament also has much to say about offering thanks as families and individuals. Paul writes to the Thessalonians, "Rejoice always. Pray without ceasing. In all circumstances give thanks, for this is the will of God for you in Christ Jesus" (1 Thess. 5:16–17). I used to read that Scripture and say to myself, "How is that possible? How can I rejoice always? How can I give thanks in all circumstances?" I realized that I didn't understand what rejoicing and thanksgiving were all about. I thought they involved a feeling of being happy, but in the biblical sense it is much deeper than feelings. Yes, there is often an element of emotion connected with rejoicing, but joy is primarily a virtue and not an emotion. It is something that we willfully choose, and we need to practice choosing joy and thanksgiving in all situations.

We are called to give thanks in all circumstances because we know that God is working in all circumstances. Thanksgiving for the believer is a response to God's saving action. God is always in our lives working out His purpose. In that light we can be a people of thanksgiving. We need to learn to confess to ourselves the goodness of God and to teach our children to do it also. Our family, like everyone else, sometimes encounters tragedy and suffering. Often, the one thing that turns our pain into joy is a thankful attitude.

Continual thanksgiving requires training for moms and dads, but also for the children. We should teach our children to thank God even in difficulties because, ultimately, we believe what the Scriptures teach. God does turn everything to good for those who love Him (Rom. 8:28), but often we are unable to see God's design. He is timeless and always has the eternal perspective in mind. We know that God wants us to live with Him forever, and so we must believe that all things happen for a reason if we have placed Him in control of our lives. In light of that, we can thank Him for every difficulty.

Corrie ten Boom, in her book *The Hiding Place,* describes several desperate situations she survived through the inspiration of her sister. I recall one story in particular that describes Corrie's and her sister, Betsy's, experience in a terrible concentration camp. Betsy was sickly, and Corrie was healthy; yet Betsy always lifted Corrie up, both spiritually and emotionally. One day when Corrie was particularly depressed and struggling, Betsy said to her, "Corrie, there is no pit too deep that God isn't deeper still." That is the mystery of breaking through with thanksgiving, of understanding that nothing, as St. Paul writes to the Romans, can separate us from the love of God in Christ (Rom. 8:38–39).

As families, we need to cultivate that attitude in our homes, teach it to our children, and demonstrate it by example. We should offer thanks to God in all circumstances. Difficult situations and painful experiences can tempt us to fall into despair, and these are the times that we must choose to give thanks and rejoice. Paul and Silas suffered terribly in chains, but amidst their suffering, they decided to praise God in prayer and song (Acts 16:25). The Scripture records:

> About midnight Paul and Silas were praying and singing hymns to God, and the other prisoners were listening to them. Suddenly there was such a violent earthquake that the foundations of the prison were shaken. At once all the prison doors flew open, and everybody's chains came loose. (Acts 16:25–26 NIV)

One of the great ways to express thanks is through song. As we rejoice in the Lord for all things, we need an outlet for all of that emotion. Singing provides a healthy release of the joy that we experience. St. Paul writes to the Ephesian Christians, "Be filled with the Spirit, addressing one another [in] psalms and hymns and spiritual songs, singing and playing to the Lord in all your hearts, giving thanks always and for everything in the name of our Lord Jesus Christ to God the Father" (Eph. 5:18b–20).

My family has found much joy in singing to the Lord, and singing has helped our prayer lives. Music has a way of pulling us beyond ourselves, freeing our minds to be open to the urgings of the Spirit. Some families will say, "No one in our house can carry a tune," but that should not matter. Our attitude should be one of praise, not performance. What matters is that we are singing to the Lord, that we are expressing our joy for His gifts.

Song is just one way to express thanksgiving, and there are so many others. We can do it through daily prayer as a family, through service to one another and our local church, through our entire lives lived with an attitude of gratitude. Something we find very helpful in our home happens around the dinner table when every member of the family, as well as any guest we may have, honors the Lord for something He has done. During our family prayer, we try to have a time every day when each of the children can thank God for something He did for them. It is important to teach the family to be thankful because when we are a people of thanksgiving we will truly become the joyful people of God.

These kinds of practices cultivate an attitude of mind and heart. It excites me to hear my children thank the Lord for the things He does for them, and it makes me realize that I often make life all too complicated. I do not always recognize that God is at work in my own mundane circumstances.

In our daily lives, when we offer all we are doing to the Lord in thanksgiving, even the difficult things, we are united in the passion of Christ. We become more like Him. Jesus who walked among us and understood everything of our human experience shows us the way to live a life of thanksgiving in complete submission and obedience to the Father's will. He experienced flesh and blood, He understands, and He was thankful through it all. I am always reminded of the return of the seventy-two when Jesus, "full of joy through the Holy Spirit," thanked the Father (Luke 10:21 NIV).

Our primary reason for thanksgiving is Christ's life, death, and resurrection. We should be grateful for salvation, especially since we did nothing to deserve it. Eternal life is God's pure gift to His people. We did nothing and can do nothing to earn salvation. The prophet Isaiah says, "Our good deeds are like polluted rags" (Isa. 64:5). We are the most privileged of people to have salvation, to have new life in Jesus Christ. Jesus says in St. Luke's Gospel, "Do not rejoice because the spirits are subject to you, but rejoice because your names are written in heaven" (Luke 10:20). We have cause for rejoicing and thanksgiving because there is a place in heaven reserved for us (1 Peter 3 and 4).

We can thank Him for His daily care. When we become anxious and confused about God's plan for our lives, remember that our ability to see the future is limited. Only God knows the outcome of our lives, and we have to trust His ways because He told us through the prophet Isaiah, "My thoughts are not your thoughts, nor are your ways my ways, says the LORD. As high as the heavens are above the earth, so high are my ways above your ways and my thoughts above your thoughts" (Isa. 55:8–9). His thoughts are always right, and He cares for every detail of our lives. We need to be grateful for His attentiveness to the details of our life.

We can thank God for all of creation. God's creation reveals His glory, especially the brilliance of a morning sunrise or evening sunset, the majesty of the mountain tops, and the mystical embrace of the ocean. St. Francis knew the glory of nature. He loved creation, because he saw within the beauty of creation, a reflection of God. He saw God's love and mercy and compassion in the flowers and the animals. He saw God bursting forth in song through the vibrancy of the colors in the October leaves and the uniqueness of each winter snowflake. We need to share with our children the wonder of God's creation. Did you ever take a walk with one of your children and join together in thanking the Lord for the beauty of the trees and the mountains. Perhaps you think that would be a little awkward, but it can be a part of our life as a family.

I once took my son Keith to a friend's cabin in Hidden Valley, nestled in the mountains of Pennsylvania. One of the highlights of the weekend was our wonder over God's revelation in nature.

Neither of us said much, but we both connected with each other and with the Lord.

We should thank God for our trials too. Now, usually this is difficult. The words of the prophet are always encouraging:

> Though the fig tree does not bud and there are no grapes on the vines, though the olive crop fails and the fields produce no food, though there are no sheep in the pen and no cattle in the stalls, yet I will rejoice in the LORD, I will be joyful in God my Savior. The Sovereign LORD is my strength; he makes my feet like the feet of a deer, he enables me to go on the heights. (Hab. 3:17–19 NIV)

The prophet can thank the Lord in all circumstances even when it seems as if there are no provisions. That is the attitude of thanksgiving the Lord wants His people to have. We should thank the Lord even in our trials, testings, and chastisements. And we should be able to teach our children to do the same. St. James writes in his epistle, "Realize that when your faith is tested this makes for endurance. Let endurance come to its perfection so that you may be fully mature and lacking in nothing" (James 1:3–4).

The Scripture teaches us this over and over again. For instance in Romans 5:3–4 Paul says, "We even boast of our afflictions, knowing that affliction produces endurance, and endurance, proven character, and proven character, hope." Again, in Hebrews 12:11 we read, "At the time it is administered, all discipline seems a cause for grief and not joy, but later it brings forth the fruit of peace and justice to those who are trained in its school."

We can thank the Lord for difficult times. Job is a great example of that. In the famous passage from the book of Job, we find Job faced with the reality that everyone had abandoned him, even his family, and he said, "Slay me though he [the Lord] might, I will wait for him; I will defend my conduct before him" (Job 13:15). I will trust Him. We need to trust Him in the difficult times and teach our children through word and example to do the same.

We have many things to be thankful for as we have seen, but most of all, let us thank the Lord for one another, for our families, and for the family of the Church. What a great privilege He has given us, to live our lives for Him in our families as the domestic church. What a privilege it is to be His instruments for one another's salvation and sanctification, to be given the opportunity as parents to train the next generation for the Lord, and for His church, and to participate with God in His creative work in the lives of our children. We have much to be thankful for.

Husbands, thank the Lord for your wives. Wives, thank the Lord for your husbands. It is great to do that aloud and to honor one another. Sacred Scripture says to "outdo one another in showing honor" (Rom. 12:10 RSV).

What does it mean to "honor" one another? Many people are completely unfamiliar with this concept for various reasons. Some may simply have never been taught. Others may feel that "my family knows how I feel; I don't need to tell them." Still others enter into the destructive habit of biting sarcasm, putting one another down in the name of humor.

My experience as a minister has shown me clearly that negative humor opens wounds and leaves scars. Many have been deeply hurt by comments their family has made to them. Family wounds leave the deepest scars. We need to let one another know how thankful we are to be a family and how thankful we are for each member, no matter what he or she has done.

We should build each other up in our speech instead of causing each other to crumble. Birthdays in particular are a great time to introduce the concept of honoring and showing how thankful we are for that person. Everyone present can say something to encourage and build the confidence and self-respect of the honoree. Feeling honored and respected on a consistent basis changes people. It makes them more self-confident, less defensive, and therefore more able to love and receive love. That's the kind of reality we want to provide for our children—being thankful for the blessing that we are for one another as the domestic church.

Let us thank the Lord as well for the gift of the whole Church, that universal sign of salvation. What a great joy we have as Christians. We should thank the Lord for Christian leaders, for fearless, prophetic leaders who speak the truth in our day. For men and women like Billy Graham, John Paul II, and Mother Teresa. We should thank Him for the wonder of the time in which we live and the challenge of the next century. But this "attitude of gratitude" will first require a change of heart

Conclusion

Thanksgiving first takes root in the heart and then works itself out into actions. We can open up to true thanksgiving only when our hearts are free from bitterness, malice, guilt, self-absorption, unforgiveness, or any thoughts that are not of God. Thanksgiving is somewhat like the culmination of the entire process of coming to terms with what God is doing in our lives.

When we rejoice in what God is doing, we are opened for His blessings to be released within us. That is why when we pray for intentions, we should thank God in advance for His answer. Thanksgiving predisposes us to what the Lord wants to do. In giving thanks, we break down any obstacles that would block God's work in our lives. We choose to trust in Him and thank Him for the outcome, whatever it is.

Thanksgiving must be part of the fabric of our family life. Our lives should reflect our thanks to God in speech, thoughts, and actions. But there is a time for showing our gratitude in specific ways. Prayer, which as we know is our lifeline to God, should always include a time of thanksgiving, of acknowledging God's gifts. Relationship cannot always be asking and receiving. We have to give, and thanksgiving is one big moment of giving, and for the Lord it must be a precious moment. He must rejoice in seeing His children appreciate the love He offers and return it with grateful hearts.

The key to all of this is our individual and family lifeline to God, prayer, the topic of our next chapter.

10

Prayer

God our Father, God our Father,
Let's begin, let's begin,
Thank You for our blessings, thank You for our blessings
Amen, amen.

It had been a hard day, a long day, and a draining day. I was ready to eat, and we had assembled around the dinner table. I wanted to rush through our blessing. However, the Lord had something else in mind. My son Joel, who was three years old at the time, wanted to pray the blessing. Out of his mouth came this little song (I have since found out that the second line is "once again"). He must have sung it four times. It struck me the third time around how very special this whole event really was. It was his first dinner blessing. I was able, by God's grace, to break out of my own self-centered irritability and recognize the sacredness of the moment. He had learned a prayer on his own. He was proud of himself. And I am sure he caused great joy in the heavenlies. He also stood in a long tradition of those who have gone on before him, who have taken time to give thanks.

My approach to the whole affair was anything but commendable. But it was fairly typical. Prayer is difficult at times, isn't it? Yet there is nothing more important to family life than prayer. The old adage of Father Patrick Peyton is absolutely true: "The family that prays together stays together." Families will live the way they pray and pray the way they live. If we are serious about seeing our families become domestic churches, we must pray. At the heart of the domestic church is the Head of the domestic church, Jesus Christ. The only way one can stay in a dynamic relationship with Him is through conversation. That conversation is called prayer.

The early church had many different elements that enabled it to be strong and to be missionary. They were convicted and disciplined in their worship, preaching, and life-style. But the most important element was the power in their prayer. Their prayer lives were dynamic, living, full of the Holy Spirit, and effective. They followed in the footsteps of their Master. The Scriptures are replete with examples of Jesus' prayer life. At every major event in His life He prayed. One of the most beautiful accounts of His prayer life is found in the first chapter of Mark, where we read, "Very early in the morning, while it was still dark, Jesus got up, left the house and went off to a solitary place, where he prayed" (Mark 1:35 NIV).

The Scriptures record that after that event He cured a man with leprosy, a paralytic, and began to call men to follow Him. He always followed this pattern. He always began his significant moments with prayer. After His baptism, Luke tells us, "Jesus, full of the Holy Spirit, returned from the Jordan and was led by the Spirit into the desert . . . for forty days" (Luke 4:1 NIV). And what did He do in the desert? He fasted, He prayed, He fought spiritual battles, and He resisted temptations. And what happened? Again we read, "[He] returned to Galilee in the power of the Spirit" (Luke 4:14 NIV).

That's what can happen to our families. And we need it, don't we?

After spending a significant amount of time in prayer, Jesus began His public ministry and began to teach. Similarly we have a teaching ministry to our children, and we need spiritual wisdom.

The early church was filled with men and women who understood the power of prayer. On the day of Pentecost, they were gathered in one place to pray and as a result, the Holy Spirit fell in power (Acts 2). The world was never the same.

Prayer is the most powerful force in the universe because it unleashes the power of the living God before which all else must fall. Through prayer we will see that power unleashed in the family. Through prayer we will see the demons flee, sin and woundedness healed and forgiven, and the mountains of ordinary struggle transformed.

John Wesley once said, "God will do nothing, but in answer to prayer." In God's infinite love and mercy, He does not force Himself upon us, but somehow has allowed us to participate in His rulership, His dominion, His creation, His redemption—through the power of prayer.

The letter of James reminds us that the great warriors of prayer, including Elijah, were human just like us. Yet the Lord worked through their prayers. I find this encouraging when I think of the incredible task of raising five children!

Doesn't it seem obvious that if we bear the name Christian we need to stay in touch with Christ? And one way families can do that is through family prayer. Prayer should be at the heart of our lives together as a family. Prayer should be a natural part of the fabric, the stuff of our daily life. When our children are ill, we should pray. When we are struggling, we should pray. When we are happy, we should pray. When we celebrate, at baptisms, first communions, confirmations, and weddings, or in difficult times, at funerals and times of deep sorrow, we should pray. And not just *say* prayers (though form prayers are a great help), but conversationally and realistically talk to God as our Father.

John Paul II speaks often about family prayer.

It should never be forgotten that prayer constitutes an essential part of Christian life, understood in its fullness and centrality. . . . Far from being a form of escapism from everyday commitments, prayer constitutes the strongest incentive for the Christian family to assume and comply fully with all of its responsibilities as the primary and fundamental cell of human society.[1]

Prayer is not a way of escape, but a way to be prepared and empowered to become the servants of God that we were created to be. Thus, the Christian family's actual participation in the Church's life and mission is in direct proportion to the fidelity and intensity of the prayer with which it is united to the fruitful vine, Jesus Christ, the Lord. "Without me you can do nothing" (John 15:5). We can do nothing in God's wisdom if we are not nourished and sustained by prayer. In as much as we pray together as a family, we will be united to Christ and to His fruitful vine, the Church.

Prayer is an important element in sustaining our responsibility as people on mission, not an escape from it. Neither is prayer a last resort—"If all else fails, *pray!*" Prayer is not something we fall back on when all other avenues have been explored. Prayer is not a desperate "Hail Mary Pass," as they say in football. We don't just heave up our difficult situations to God and hope that by some miracle all comes out well. This is not what faith entails. Instead, "Faith is the realization of what is hoped for and evidence of things not seen" (Heb. 11:1). Faith is believing that our prayer makes a difference to God, that He chose for it to make a difference. Faith is trusting God's provision in answer to our prayer even when circumstances seem hopeless.

Another false adage we hear from the secular realm is "God helps those who help themselves." This is a bit more subtle because it draws upon our healthy desire to be responsible adults. Seeds of truth are embedded in this deception. It's true that the grace of God cooperates with our nature. It is dangerous to become so superspiritual that we forget our natural role in relationship with God. On the other hand, that familiar saying is systematically incorrect at the root. It comes dangerously close to an Aristotelian notion of God as First Mover, who set all things into motion and let them go, a theory that does not allow for God's intervention in our lives or for the power of prayer.

If children learn and practice prayer in their families, these lessons will continue through eternity. If the family does not pray, it cannot be a domestic church. In a 1980 homily, John Paul II said,

As a "Church in miniature," sacramentally founded, or a domestic church, marriage and the family must be a school of faith and a place of common prayer. I attribute great significance precisely to prayer in the family. It gives strength to overcome many problems and difficulties.[2]

We won't be able to live out our call and vocation without prayer. We need the power of God. We need to pray. Taking into account the realities of our lives, the realities of the age of our children, the realities of the pressure of the contemporary days we live in, we need to resolve that we are going to be a people of prayer, that we are going to be the praying domestic church.

With all of the different commitments that need attention in our families, we need to be flexible but consistent in developing a prayer life in our family. We should realize that if we have young children, there is a certain way we should plan our schedule that conforms with their age and their ability to grasp the truth of faith and prayer. If we have teenage children, similarly, we need to make adjustments. Rigidity can be the greatest enemy.

Teenagers respond completely differently than the younger children. They have discovered a whole new world outside the home—friends, school activities, sports, parties, football games, dances, etc. Their world is filled with their own needs and desires. Developmentally, they are dealing with being accepted by others, learning to relate in new ways, trusting people other than family, competing in and out of school, growing physically, making decisions, and taking on more responsibility. A whole host of emotions shape our children at this stage. They cannot be expected to have personal and family prayer as top priority at this age. This kind of expectation only pressures them and frustrates us.

On the other hand, part of training our children is making them responsible for things that they may not want to do. That's all part of growing up. Balancing this tension is the most delicate process a Christian parent faces. Flexibility is crucial. Forcing on our children a daily prayer time at a specific hour may launch them into rebellion instead of helping them to form a good habit. Consequently they may begin to rebel at the thought of prayer and even the thought of God. Eternal realities are light years away from the invincible youth. Nothing matters to him or her except the now moment.

Parents need to be flexible through the crazy stages of the teenage years. We can encourage them to have a daily time of personal prayer, but it doesn't usually work if we demand that they do so. Teens should, however, be responsible for participating in some form of family prayer. Here is where consistency becomes important. Moms and Dads, consistent family prayer is critical for the domestic church. Acts 2 tells us the structure of the early church, but does not show each member doing his own thing. No, it reads, "All who believed were together" (Acts 2:44). Moreover, the writer of the letter to the Hebrews warns the early Christians, "Do not forsake the assembly of the brethren." These warnings apply to the domestic church as well. Prayer is the life blood of the Church. Just as without blood, human beings could not exist, without prayer, the domestic church flounders and dies.

Prayer must be scheduled into daily life. We all know what happens when we leave prayer for "later in the day when I have time." It never happens. Family prayer is a constant challenge. Getting everyone together at the same time, trying to ignore who is in a bad mood or tired, trying to be patient with the little ones who can ramble forever. I know that Joel will move beyond his sung blessing at meals. He already has. And in keeping with the brothers and sisters who have preceded him, he now rambles in a stream-of-consciousness approach to prayer. It's tough, but forming the pattern and remaining consistent will help the family have quality time together, seeking the Lord as a body of believers.

We have found our children's response to family prayer amazing, especially the younger ones. MaryEllen and Joel, our two youngest (ages five and three) love to be involved. They are generally the last to pray because we have found that order in prayer (oldest to youngest) is helpful. Inevitably, however, Joel will chime in with, "My turn, my turn!" Now, Joel is only three years old and cognitively does not really understand what he is doing, but the point is that he is identifying and participating with the body and building up the domestic church.

Again, flexibility needs to be a part of family prayer. Change will forever be a part of our lives. Learning how to adjust to change makes things a whole lot easier. For example, my family used to set aside time after dinner to share the day and pray together, and we had personal prayer times first thing in the morning. This worked fairly well for a few years, but during the summers, everything went haywire. The kids slept later, they were out all day, some stayed for dinner at friends' homes, the neighborhood played softball immediately after dinner every night, everyone came home exhausted. Summer is a whole other reality. We find it necessary to regularly adjust and readjust our schedule. We find it helpful to bring our children into the process of scheduling, to get their input. This way they don't feel imposed upon. Rather, they feel that they have helped make the decision about family matters. They have become personally involved and so they more easily take ownership of the commitment.

The temptation in family prayer is to give up trying. But the most important thing is *not* to give up praying together. Seize the natural opportunities for prayer: illness, celebration, needs. We should not only reach for a pain medication when illness strikes, but freely lay hands on each other and pray.

How Should We Pray?

When John Paul II toured America in 1987, he said this:

Prayer begins in the home. The prayers that serve us well in life are often those learned at home when we were children. But prayer in the home also serves to introduce the children to liturgical prayer of the whole Church; it helps to apply the Church's prayer to everyday events, and to the special moments of a family's experience.[3]

Do you remember some of the prayers you learned as a child? I do. Night prayer was always the same—"Now I lay me down to sleep. I pray the Lord my soul to keep. If I should die before I wake, I pray the Lord my soul to take." Although a child's prayer, those words are packed with important teaching. The prayer shows trust in the Lord, knowledge that God is in control, a basic understanding of the afterlife, and a desire to spend eternity with God.

That simple prayer also taught me the importance of seeking God in prayer before I go to bed. I now try to pray compline, the night prayer of the Liturgy of the Hours when I can, which is exactly what the Pope in the above quote predicts will happen—"Prayer in the home also serves to introduce the children to liturgical prayer of the whole Church."

The most obvious example of this is, of course, the liturgy itself, which is prefigured by both a daily offering to God and the prayer before the meal. Growing up Catholic, my parents taught us the daily form prayers. Laurine and I have tried to teach our kids to "give the day to the Lord" in their own words. It sets priorities straight and calls for the grace and power they need. The daily offering teaches our kids that everything, even their difficulties and struggles, can be offered up to the Lord where their suffering can be joined to the passion of the cross.

The prayer before meals can take various forms. One common form is as follows: "Bless us, O Lord, and these Thy gifts, which we are about to receive from Thy bounty through Christ our Lord, Amen." Or, the prayer offered on the first Thanksgiving by Governor Bradford: "Lord God, come before us as we ask Thy blessing. Thy hand has watchfully brought us to this land. . . . We do give solemn thanks and praise to Thy name." On the surface these prayers give thanksgiving for earthly food and provision, but the deeper goal is to point to the real food, the heavenly food of the Lord Himself, given to us in His Word, one another, and His holy Meal, the Eucharist.

We try to take the opportunity to make these connections for our children and to make sure that they understand *why* we pray the way we do. They will not understand and do not need to know the theology behind all of their prayers, but they need to know the power in it.

Did you ever feel like you just couldn't pray? I have. Most of the time I feel too tired or stressed or emotional or I just don't have anything to say or I can't for the life of me focus on the Lord. Well, if we adults have these problems, rest assured our children do! So how can we help them form habits in these early years? What can we teach them about prayer? Fortunately God in His goodness has made it easy for us to reach Him. He has planned it so that we can reach Him by nearly any means. But we have to put forth some effort too. We have to be willing to be alone with God.

Personal prayer time is often difficult or dry for adults, let alone children with short attention spans. But the Lord has provided for us a plethora of tools to enter into prayer. Formal prayers for instance are a wonderful blessing, and there are many of them. We should teach our children and develop in our home fresh expressions of piety and devotion, plumbing the wealth of the treasures of the Church—the Scriptures.

While we encourage our children to pray, my wife and I try not to place too much responsibility on the kids. We prefer they become familiar with prayer as a conversation with God and talk to Him regularly.

I remember feeling astounded when a wise grade school teacher of mine, Sister William Patricia, told me that I could talk to Jesus anywhere at any time. She taught me that I could say prayers, but that I also could just talk to Him. That had a great impact on my life. Some of the most comforting moments of my early years were when I would take the time to just talk to God.

For our children, the same can be true. They can experience God in their need by calling on Him, being honest with their feelings, and waiting for His comfort. If this type of relationship is ever going to blossom between our children and the Lord, we need to allow them to be creative in their prayer. Too much structure kills spontaneity with God. I have to be willing to allow my son Joel to babble on and on, even if I don't feel like listening. I have to be willing to allow one of my daughters to be angry with God and to tell Him so. I have to be willing to allow them to take a break from reading Scripture if they cannot concentrate. I as a father need to allow my children to become comfortable in the presence of God and to develop their own relationship with Him, not a carbon copy of mine.

Within formal prayer time, we believe Scripture study is invaluable. The Scriptures are the words of life, the wisdom of the ages. God will speak to us if we become vulnerable to His Word. Countless times, God has used the Scriptures to inspire me, exhort me, comfort me, or help me makes sense of a situation. Similarly God has been faithful in speaking to my children through His Word. Give your children the gift of the Bible; show them by your own example how the Word of God changes people.

Within the context of family prayer, we use Scripture. Often taking the great evangelical tradition as our model. In speaking of the early evangelical movement, *The Westminster Dictionary of Christian Spirituality* says, "Family prayers were expected to take place in every evangelical household, the head of the household calling his family and servants together every morning and evening and reading a portion of the Scripture before the prayers."[4] Wouldn't it be wonderful if this were said of *our* homes!

Spiritual reading other than the Bible helps tremendously in private prayer for both adults and children. Reading inspirational works from great leaders of the Christian faith helps us know what these men and women of God experienced and how they responded. For my children, reading the lives of great Christians always inspires them.

Repeat After Me

So we've got to break our children into these patterns, but sometimes the most difficult part is just getting started. In our home with each of the children in their early years, we have used the "Repeat after me," technique. As fathers and mothers we have the great privilege to say, "Repeat after me: Lord Jesus," "Lord Jesus," "I love you," "I love you. . . ." You see, through our words we teach them how to tap into the Spirit within them and then that same Spirit will guide them in a life of prayer. Children are very quick and, therefore, though this technique is short-lived, it is a beginning.

Do we ever really grow up from this, though? Look at some of the great leaders of the Christian church. They use this technique as a primary component of evangelization and repentance. Billy Graham during an altar call with "Just as I Am" playing in the background; Pat Robertson on the TV screen during the "700 Club"—these men and countless others realize the power in teaching others how to pray, especially children in the faith who lack experience.

In my own tradition, this technique is also used. Often while attending Mass in a large church in Steubenville, Ohio, the congregation was led by the priest in a time of repentance and renewal of commitment to Christ. Something happens during those moments. There is a surge of power released within us as we again decide for Christ, and the fruit is joy. This is what the "profession of faith" in the Catholic liturgy is supposed to be: an opportunity to reaffirm our baptismal promises.

Intercession

We should also teach our children other important aspects of Christian prayer. Have we taught our children how to intercede, not only out of their own needs, but out of the heart of Christ who dwells within them? God has shown us how important it is to pray for one another in our home. The Word of God says, "In everything, by prayer and petition, with thanksgiving make your requests known to God" (Phil. 4:6). Our experience as a family hasn't been consistent in this, but we have set it as a continual goal.

Self-denial

Have we brought our children into spiritual disciplines, such as fasting? Sometimes we think children ought not be involved in fasting. Well, depending on their age, we can involve them in some portion of sacrifice because Christianity is a life of sacrifice, a life of selflessness, a life of self-denial.

The early Christians were quite at home with sacrifice, and their willingness to suffer released tremendous power in their prayer and missionary effort. Peter's letters were written to dispersed Christians undergoing persecution. He told them, "Therefore, since Christ suffered in his body, arm yourselves also with the same attitude" (1 Peter 4:1 NIV).

Power of the Cross

In my tradition as a Catholic Christian, I have been taught since my earliest childhood to make the sign of the cross as a symbol of my dedication to Christ. My wife and I have also taught our children from their very early days to use that great sign by which we are all sealed, the Sign of the Cross. I found it a blessing to teach the Sign of the Cross to my children. It was a joy for me to trace the cross on them and teach them to use the Sign of the Cross. MaryEllen, now five, fumbled for weeks, flailing her hands off center or wide to the right or left. But she somehow knew that action was important to do. Now three years later, an expert at this point, she now automatically (and deftly, I might add) seals herself with that powerful sign. What a great privilege to teach her through a physical symbol the fundamental truth of her life. She has been saved by the cross and she now belongs to Christ. There is great power in that cross for her life, for all our lives.

The Joy of the Lord Is Our Strength

All of these structures are helpful, but quiet time must always be balanced with a fervent joy in the Lord, especially for the children. They need to know that prayer is not just a task, but something they can have fun doing. Singing is a powerful way to bring our children into prayer. St. Augustine said, "He who sings, prays twice." I think it does please the heart of God to hear us singing.

My family loves to sing. We encourage our children to sing in their prayer time and to use musical instruments. We try to have Christian music in our home, particularly music that puts the Scripture to song. It is wonderful to hear the children, even before they can read, singing the Word of God as they go about the house. I love to hear my children, full of energy, singing a rousing rendition of a favorite song.

If they learn songs that are scriptural, whenever they begin to sing these songs, in a special way they enter into the presence of God. I love when my children sing to the Lord because I know that if it pleases my heart, then it must please the heart of their Father in heaven.

Praise and worship raises our spirit to God. Praise can change our mood. Praise can pull us out of self-centeredness and position us before the throne of God. It helps us to release the cares, tensions, and distractions of the day and focus on the Lord. Our children need to learn to open up to God in worship and praise. Undoubtedly they will at first feel awkward and self-conscious. I think everyone experiences that. But if you enter into uninhibited praise with your children, they will eventually see it as the ordinary way to begin prayer.

Repentance

We have examined the need for private prayer and praise, but I also want to emphasize the importance of teaching the family prayers of repentance. At times in our family prayer, we have had a time of repentance when the events of the day warranted it. From these times our children can learn the reality of sin and the fact that sin grieves God and offends the Body of Christ. They need to learn how to get free from sin: to acknowledge it, to confess it, and to give it over to the Lord so that He can set them free. They also need to know that it has a personal and corporate dimension.

I think it is critical in this generation that we teach our children the reality of sin. We live in a time when people excuse, justify, or ignore the implications of sin. Some contemporary thinkers, in the name of "freedom of conscience," lead our children into bondage. Freedom of conscience is wonderful if seen in its proper light and not distorted by people who want to rationalize a destructive and sinful life-style. The way to freedom is to acknowledge our sin and be saved from it through the blood of Jesus Christ. As Catholics, when the children are old enough, they participate fully in that great sacrament of second chance, the Sacrament of Penance and Reconciliation.

We all need to experience healing of the wound, the severed relationship between the sinner and God, but also between the sinner and the Church. We teach our children that, as members of the Body of Christ, anything they do affects the entire body. But God alone forgives their sin, the moment they ask. Teaching them that profound but simple truth is one of the most important things a Christian parent can do, no matter what tradition he or she belongs to. In an age of bondage, it is the key to their freedom.

More Ways to Pray As a Family

There are many formal devotions in my own tradition that focus on the saving events of our faith. If you are not used to form prayers, you may want to establish some within your own tradition. What is most important about any such approach to prayer and reflection is that it gives God the time to teach us about the Incarnation, the Crucifixion, the Resurrection and many of the other great wonders of our faith. For us, traditional novenas (nine days of concentrated prayer and reflection) are a great blessing. Far from being outdated, a novena can be a source of great power and freshness for a family that is serious about being the domestic church. We find it helpful to allow our children to lead the meditations. It gives them a chance to express what God is teaching them and to feel part of the prayer in a special way. We particularly rely on this form of prayer during great Church seasons, such as Lent, Pentecost, and Christmas.

There are other special times of prayer that are possible for the family. For example, on certain Saturday mornings years ago when my children were younger and my schedule permitted, my son and I would get together with some of the men from our parish and their sons. We would have a "father-son" prayer room. Our sons looked forward to the morning meetings because it gave them a sense of belonging. My wife, too, would often get together with our daughters and sometimes with other women for similar prayer times. We have other occasions as well when we join our families with others to pray. These times illustrate for our children the importance of stepping outside the confines of the family and welcoming time with the community of believers. When we pray together, one domestic church with another, we build up the larger Church and become missionary in our very presence. Strengthening each other, building up the Church, and worshiping God in spirit and in truth—isn't that what it means to be church?

All of this is our effort to respond to the call of the Lord and the clear teaching of the Christian church that, as families, the domestic church, we need to pray; we need to live a life of prayer. John Paul II says this:

The church prays for the Christian family and educates the family to live in generous accord with the priestly gift and role received from Christ the high priest. In effect, the baptismal priesthood of the faithful exercised in the Sacrament of Marriage constitutes the basis of a priestly vocation and mission for the spouses and family by which their daily lives are transformed into "spiritual sacrifices acceptable to God through Jesus Christ."[5]

We who live out our response to God in family also have a role in the priestly ministry of Christ. We parents especially must offer our children to the Lord in prayer. "Family prayer has for its very own object family life itself."[6] In other words, you cannot really experience the fullness of family life without family prayer.

Family is seen as a call from God. Do we realize that? Do we realize that living out our family life is a response to a call? Joys and sorrows, hopes and disappointments, births and birthday celebrations, wedding anniversaries, departures, homecomings, important and far-reaching decisions, the death of those who are dear—all of these mark God's loving intervention in family history. They should be seen as suitable moments for thanksgiving, for petition, for abandonment of the family into the hands of their Father. We will only gain dignity and fulfillment as the domestic church as we seek God's constant help in daily, humble prayer.

In our daily life, we who are in families experience ups and downs, trials and difficulties, joys and times of celebration. All of these can be accompanied by prayer, prayers of thanksgiving, prayers of celebration, prayers of intercession, prayers of repentance, prayers of sorrow and mourning before the Lord.

Eternal Prayer

We need to become comfortable with this kind of thing in the home and to develop a habit of prayer. Did you ever think about being with the Lord for eternity praying and worshiping Him? I think God allows us to learn how to pray on earth so that we will not suffer from culture shock when we reach heaven. If we pray now and get comfortable with thanksgiving and praise, we will be ready for the high courts.

Read the book of Revelation and see what the Church does in heaven. A key passage from John's vision appears in Revelation 5:

> Then I saw standing in the midst of the throne . . . a Lamb that seemed to have been slain. . . . He came and received the scroll from the right hand of the one who sat on the throne. When he took it, the four living creatures and the twenty-four elders fell

down before the Lamb. Each of the elders held a harp and gold bowl filled with incense, which are the prayers of the holy ones. They sang a new hymn. (vv. 6–9)

John is describing here the liturgy of the heavens, the very form of worship that we imitate in a small way during our lifetimes. Liturgy is God's form of worship, not something that structures our communal prayer on earth. Revelation hints that heaven will be one continual, powerful liturgy. Constant prayer, eternal praise—that is what we will be doing and what our children will be doing. That is why we begin now with our children. There is a paraliturgical dimension in the home. In other words, the events that occur in Christian liturgy, and indeed in heaven, occur in a symbolic way in our homes—worship, prayer, sacrifice, celebration. As parents, we need to always take care to draw out that dimension of family life.

Let us join the heavenly hosts and make our earthly lives examples of constant prayer and praise of our Lord. Let us raise up prayer warriors within our homes. Let us lead our families to become living vessels of prayer and praise, living stones building up the Body of Christ. Let us pray.

11

Faith in the Home

"God bless Nana and Grandpa and help them to get through their problems and really know that You love them." It was Annie's turn to pray her intercession. She was only six at the time, and in her characteristic six-year-old fervor, she did so with enthusiasm, fully convinced that she was talking to a loving Father in heaven who would not only hear her, but would also intervene in Nana and Grandpa's lives. And He did! Why? Because Annie exercised her faith, and God responds to faith.

Annie trusted with the faith of a child. Jesus told us to become like little children (Matt. 18:3). What does He actually mean? I believe He means that we are to be as vulnerable and trusting with God as children are with other people. An infant allows a complete stranger to hold and kiss him. He allows others to feed him and to care for his needs. So be it in our relationship with God. Annie gave God permission to care for the lives of her grandparents.

During this particular church season, we had assigned a specific intention to Annie and to all of our children. We asked them to pray until they saw a change in the situation or the person for whom they were praying. Even MaryEllen (who was three at the time) got an assignment, and daily she prayed. . . and in the most unique ways. (Happily God interprets!) Our family's involvement in intercessory prayer was and is one way that Laurine and I try to foster a dynamic, living faith in our home. Interceding as a body of believers, exercising faith as a community is not reserved for church services. Faith needs to be built every day in our homes.

Obviously faith had to be the key component, the glue that held the early church together. Imagine the early Christians who were faced with the "impossible" reality of Jesus' rising from the dead. The concept is mind-boggling for us, and we have had centuries of predecessors making sense of it for us. Not so for the first-century Christians. They had to believe in something radically new and frankly ridiculous. But they did and they exercised faith in that "impossible" truth day in and day out.

Belief

"All who *believed* were together" (Acts 2:44, emphasis added). Belief is fundamental. As Christians, we are called to believe in a whole host of unexplainable, indefinable truths. God the Father, God the Son, God the Holy Spirit are three Persons in one God. Jesus Christ is the Son of God—fully human, fully divine. Mary of Nazareth, a virgin, conceived Jesus through the power of the Holy Spirit. Jesus Christ was crucified for our sins, but on the third day, He rose from the dead. Jesus sent the Holy Spirit upon the Church to unite them and empower them with missionary zeal. These are the fundamental truths of the faith that our children need to believe and need to trust.

God has planned and raised up family life as the ordinary vehicle to lead to salvation and sanctification. Our families possess the same Holy Spirit as the early church, and He brings unity and power to the domestic church. Faith in all of these truths is the power that transforms a family into a domestic church.

Faith is something we need to impart to our children—a knowledge of the faith and a living experience of it. Parents are responsible for guiding and teaching their children, for raising them in faith—believing in God, in His protection and Fatherhood, His love, His call for each of them. That relationship as son or daugh-

165

ter of God is the foundation of faith. Faith is a response to that relationship. Yes is the perfect response to God.

The author of Hebrews writes, "without faith it is impossible to please him, for anyone who approaches God must believe that he exists and that he rewards those who seek him" (Heb. 11:6). Faith calls us to believe that He exists in every moment and in each event in our lives. Without faith, we cannot please God or live holy lives. Why? Faith is the bridge between God and humanity. Faith allows God to move and transform our families. Faith gives freedom to God's expressive love. Receiving that love and expressing it back to Him pleases God.

What Is Faith?

The first thing we need to establish is what we mean by faith. The Scriptures tell us that "faith . . . is the evidence of things not seen" (Heb. 11:1). Faith is equated here with evidence. Faith is our evidence, our tangible proof that God is at work in our lives. In other words, for the believer, faith in God supplants the need to see, hear, or touch God. Eventually when we believe, we no longer need tangible signs of evidence because faith itself becomes the evidence. We walk by faith, the Scripture tells us, and not by sight. In the wonderful account of the disciple Thomas, the Lord Jesus reveals His heart to Thomas and all of us who would follow in His path: "Have you come to believe because you have seen me? Blessed are those who have not seen and have believed" (John 20:29).

As a trial lawyer, I thoroughly enjoy the arena of the courtroom with all of its drama and trial tactics. However, no matter how brilliant the presentation, a case cannot stand without evidence. I recall an experience as a young attorney that brought home for me the importance of evidence. A case of major importance was directed to my firm, and I thought it had all that a lawyer would need. The parties were believable and amiable, there was legitimate serious injury and expense, and there had been an obvious wrong that cried out for justice.

When my partner and I convened to discuss whether to take the case, I rambled on about how exciting it was. He, being older, more experienced, and weathered by courtroom battles said, "Keith, it's got everything but the evidence." And he was right. Theories and justice do not win lawsuits; tangible, physical evidence does.

Similarly theology and philosophy do not please God unless accompanied by evidence of belief. So when the Scripture tells us to please God by our faith, it refers not only to an internal or intellectual assent to the things of God, but also to a demonstration. Traditional Christian spirituality has always referred to this kind of demonstration as an "act of faith," our response not to the visible, but to the invisible.

Two of the simplest examples of such acts of faith are to praise God in the midst of adversity and to give to His work when the budget is tight. Both actions demonstrate an internal disposition of trust in His providence. They also release His power in our lives.

Valid Expressions of Faith

Our faith manifests itself in many different valid forms. There is "providential faith" that trusts in God's daily intervention in our lives. The Word of God says, "Do not worry about your life, what you will eat [or drink], or about your body, what you will wear. . . . Look at the birds in the sky; they do not sow or reap, they gather nothing into barns, yet your heavenly Father feeds them. Are not you more important than they?" (Matt. 6:25–26). This passage underscores the fundamental message of the gospel, the unconditional love of God as our Father. He is overwhelmingly concerned about absolutely everything in each of our lives. Far from the distant God of theory, He is closer than a brother or an earthly parent. Building his kind of confidence in our children will give them great security.

Providential faith is built up by stories of what God has done in other peoples' lives. In our home we also try to regularly give "testimony" to our kids of how God has acted in our individual lives and as a married couple. As the children get older, we also try to share our own story of how God rescued us. This was very effective a few years ago in Kristen's life. Her mom took her to lunch and shared her story of God's action in her life.

We also invite our children to share how God has helped them. We have had some very exciting results hearing about Jesus' healing our three year old when he wasn't even sick! But what a great way to start a lifelong habit of honoring God.

Another valid form of faith can be called "expectant faith," the faith that expects God to act. We must distinguish between expectancy and presumption, though. We can expect God to be faithful to His promises. If He has promised to provide for our needs (Matt. 6), He will. If God has said, "If you confess with your mouth Jesus is Lord, and believe in your heart that God raised him from the dead, you will be saved" (Rom. 10:9), will He not be faithful? Does that mean anyone who says, "Jesus is Lord," will be saved? No! That's not the promise. The other half of the contingency is believing in the heart. Whatever it means for each person, when we embrace the belief in our heart that Jesus was raised from the dead and are unafraid to publicly proclaim that truth, we are promised eternal life.

Many Christians, particularly in my own Catholic tradition, are uncomfortable with expecting this promise to be ultimately fulfilled. Again, we do not presume upon God something other than He has established. But it makes sense to rely on the assurances He has given to build our trust and to strengthen our faith. We expect God to be God because God can be nothing less than His perfect Self. If we truly believe that God has our best interest at heart, then we will be able to expect Him to work in our lives and act on faith in that conviction.

The danger in this area is an arrogance that we actually know what is best for us, even more than God. That is really what we are saying when we become angry, frustrated, or impatient with God when He does not do what we think He should. The problem is often that we have decided what our needs are and how they should be met. Perhaps God's plan for our provision is something we never imagined. Do we give Him the room to fulfill His promise in the most perfect way? We need to trust that God is working all things for good (Rom. 8:28)—*His* good, which is also always our good, even when we cannot see the end. We can expect that our loving Father allows all things to happen for our growth in holiness and character. Our children need to know this truth. We build for them a false and dangerous reality when we imply that God answers all of our desires. He answers all prayer, but not all desire. We try to teach our children to pray for and have faith in God's desire for their lives and help them make the distinctions as they are able. This is not easy, but neither is Christian living.

Dangerous Visions

Many other valid visions of faith exist, but along with these come some popular misinterpretations of faith that we want to avoid and not pass on to our children.

In our day, particularly, there are approaches that are actually quite dangerous, that fall short of a true biblical understanding of faith. The kind of faith that sacred Scripture talks about and to which the Church exhorts us is a faith in God, not in circumstances.

Be wary of a faith that promises all good in the present, a sort of "realized eschatology." Often this approach is expressed in statements like, "You have a right to the abundance of the earth. After all, it all belongs to God and you are His heir. You are a King's kid." This kind of thinking deceives because it is grounded in a seed of truth, but although dressed up in spiritual jargon, it can be nothing more than self-centeredness. The prophet Isaiah tells us in chapter 64:5, "Our good deeds are like polluted rags." It was by God's grace, favor, and mercy that we were given salvation through Jesus. It is true—we have been promised an everlasting inheritance. We are heirs to the kingdom of heaven. But the kingdom of heaven will not be fully realized until the coming of the Son of Man. We are permitted a foretaste of this future glory, a glimpse into the beatific vision, but not the fullness of it. We will be called to suffer at times in this world or to do without certain comforts. This is part of the Christian life. Being faithful to God through the struggles increases our faith. We begin to rely less on self with our gifts and talents and more on God's mercy and love.

It is easy to fall into thinking of "our rights." Many think that as Christians, we have the right to a good life, to financial security, to a family bursting with holiness. One difficulty with this attitude is the focus. God is not really number one; my comfort is. Faith turned inward. This preoccupation with self is actually a subtle form of idolatry, and we know the reward for idolatry. And this is a part of our human nature that is difficult to overcome. Often as we teach our children the life of faith, they quickly start praying for their own needs first, for toys or clothes or whatever. This may seem innocent, but if we fail to instruct them to move beyond themselves as they mature, a pattern can begin that will lead to an incorrect approach to faith. Teach them to pray for the desires of their heart, but always in submission to God's will.

One of the worst misinterpretations of faith posits that Christians should live in affluence and wealth all of the time. If we are to follow the example of Christ, we must look at the life of Christ. Quite obviously extreme wealth does not square with the portrait of the Son of Man who had nowhere to lay His head. Jesus had all of His needs met, but He never sought material wealth; in fact, He spoke against material wealth as an end in itself or a basis of trust. In the letter to the Hebrews we read, "Let your life be free from love of money but be content with what you have" (Heb. 13:5).

We must of course be responsible for providing for our families, but we, like Jesus, need to be satisfied with having our needs met. We ought to learn to be content with what we have. We are strangers and pilgrims on this earth, and our full reward will come in heaven. Children must learn not to lust after the things of this world, but to hunger and thirst for righteousness and truth, and to have faith that God will provide for their needs—to live as pilgrims, knowing that we have "no lasting city" (Heb. 13:14). This eternal perspective enables us to live sacrificially, individually and as a family. Our reward is eternal life. If we can impart this kind of love of heaven to our children, they will surpass us in virtue and carry the banner of Christ to the next generation.

Put to the Test

There is another misinterpretation that goes something like this: "God has given you the power of the Holy Spirit to get rid of all difficulties in your life. When you have difficulties, you can pray them away." That is not true! We have been given the power of the Holy Spirit to transform us into the image of Jesus Christ and make us holy and useful for the Church. Our transformation and preparation for mission often comes about not by getting rid of struggle, but precisely by walking through it. We need to see beneath the pain of the moment to find the good toward which the Lord is moving us. The truth is that God turns everything to good for those who love Him, but it is *His* good and it works out in the circumstances of our lives in *His* perfect timing.

The contemporary age misunderstands "good," often equating "good" with freedom from difficulty or hardship. If we think this way, none of us will be able to endure trouble and persecution. As Paul reminds us, "This momentary light affliction is producing for us an eternal weight of glory (2 Cor. 4:17).

This misunderstanding of good can come from a false concept of what it means to be a son or daughter of God. We are children of God. What is the proper response within the context of that relationship? How do children respond to their human parents? We teach them to respond with love, respect, and trust. Our reaction as sons and daughters of God should be no different. Our response is wholehearted faith, and it doesn't come automatically. We must learn it.

Faith is intimately connected with trust, but the two are different. Faith is a learned response and is based on trust. Trust, on the other hand, is something that is inborn. Children trust. Mistrust is learned from being hurt or from fear of the unknown. Generally the wounds and fear make trust extremely difficult. We even have difficulty trusting our heavenly Father sometimes. For adults, it is unnatural to be vulnerable, to relinquish control, to trust that someone outside of self knows what is best for me.

Trusting God in times of difficulty is probably the most difficult act of faith. Coincidentally it is also the most powerful witness for our children. When they see that our hope is in the Lord, they learn to respond similarly. Laurine and I have tried to show our children how to trust in the most difficult times. For instance, any time we move into a new house, we pray as a family for guidance and provision. At times, we have shared financial difficulties with our older children and asked them to pray with us. We invite the children into this prayer not to burden them, but to build their faith. They step out and trust God's provision, and when they see Him provide, their faith is bolstered. We rejoice then as a family in the faithfulness of our God. The goal for us as parents is to impart to our children an attitude of trust, a living faith that will help them respond to all circumstances. An experience of faith is an experience of trust.

Children need to learn very early the value of trust. When they trust their parents' wisdom, they will more easily trust God. We learn to build on the trust of our infancy by practicing trust with one another. Practically we call upon our children to exercise faith according to the capacity of their experience.

Just after we moved to Virginia, our son's fifth-grade teacher called us in for a meeting with the principal. They indicated that Keith's test scores and abilities were far beyond the fifth grade, and they recommended that he move on to the sixth. After much discussion and prayer, Laurine and I presented the situation to Keith. He felt both affirmed and afraid. He needed to make up his mind before the next grading period, so I spent a Saturday afternoon with him to help him decide. At the end of a hamburger, movie, and ride through the country, I asked Keith what he wanted to do. I had shared my thoughts, but now it was his turn. "Well, Dad," he said, "I want to, but I'm afraid." This gave me another opportunity to share with Keith about trusting God. He did and he made the move. Now he is flourishing and his faith has grown.

Trusting in His divine providence brings peace, and calling upon His name brings victory over trials and struggles—sometimes through their removal, sometimes through our perseverance. Experiencing true victory in Jesus strengthens and builds our character more and more into His likeness. Trials are at times necessary because they produce perseverance, and perseverance produces proven character (James 1:3ff). Even human wisdom—what we might call common sense—knows that if you only give children what they want, the end result is selfish, spoiled, unhappy children. But when they work and accomplish on their own, they mature and grow in responsibility. The same is true with faith. The more struggle they endure, the more their faith becomes like fire-purified gold. I recently heard Larry Lea speak of struggles in the Christian life. He said something very profound that touched my spirit: "Our difficult moments, rather than becoming our tombstones, can become our stepping stones." He's right

St. Paul on Suffering

One of the most misinterpreted and misquoted writers of the New Testament is St. Paul. Many use his words in an attempt to prove that the more faith you have the less struggle you will experience. I find it interesting, however, that when St. Paul's apostleship was challenged by the Corinthian Christians, he defended his position by pointing to difficulties as a sign of his authenticity (2 Cor. 11:24–27). He talks about shipwreck and hardship, being whipped, beaten, maltreated, betrayed, and left for dead. Who had more faith than Paul? Yet these are the things that proved Paul's relationship with God and his authority in the Lord. Why? Because he understood that all of us are called to share in the mystery of the suffering of the passion of Christ. He embraced the pain and was continually purified by it.

We all have difficulties. It is part of our lives and will be part of our children's lives. On a recent business trip, when I called home, I found out that my mother-in-law was diagnosed as having had several strokes and that she would need surgery. Unknown to us, she also had optical problems. Amid the seriousness of the situation, I found encouragement in my wife's response of faith. Her faith dictated her actions, and as a result, her confidence in God was strengthened. I know the children learned from their mother's example. Laurine did not exhibit even a moment of fear, just trust. She and I knew that she belonged at her mother's side, so she traveled to Louisiana and helped her mother begin her recovery. Laurine also showed tremendous peace in the midst of her own illness recently. Her perseverance and trust spoke volumes more to our family and friends than any lecture. And God has healed her.

While we can pray that difficulties be taken away, we should also pray to understand them and embrace them if that is God's will for us. In this context difficulties, struggles, and trials can become redemptive. By offering up our struggles we can "fill up what is lacking in the afflictions of Christ" (Col. 1:24). Faith, again, does not take away pain, but brings meaning and depth to it. Are we teaching our children that kind of worldview and "faithview"? If we are not, we cannot prepare them for the times that lie ahead.

This approach to struggle is not only realistic; it is biblical. What do we do? First, we pray and ask the Lord to take these things away. If He doesn't, then we ask Him to give us the strength to endure them and offer them to Him. That is faith. That is the kind of faith that changes lives and circumstances. That is the kind of faith we should be teaching our children.

How Much Faith Do I Need?

There is a wonderful passage in Matthew's Gospel where Jesus talks about just how much faith we need. He says, "I assure you, if you had faith the size of a mustard seed you would be able to say to this mountain, 'Move from here to there,' and it would move. Nothing will be impossible for you" (Matt. 17:20).

That passage never meant much to me because I had never seen a mustard seed. I often used mustard, but I had never seen the seed. I think finally seeing the tininess of that seed helped me to understand what the Lord is trying to tell us. Jesus said that we only need a tiny bit of faith to dramatically change our lives.

If faith the size of a mustard seed is enough to move a mountain, imagine the power we have as baptized Christians! Although faith is a gift, it is also a fruit of the Holy Spirit. That mustard seed grows into fruit. But remember, growth is a process. That seed has to first grow roots, then sprout, and then bloom. The faithfulness that Paul speaks of in Galatians 5:22 is cultivated over time. Practice in exercising this gift will help it blossom. How can we become a family of faith, a faithful, faith-filled family? How can we teach and train our children to respond in faith?

Faith in the Family

We can have this type of true, active faith because it is based on a knowledge of who God is and the revelation of His nature. Such knowledge leading to faith can only come if we parents, with our children, grow in our love for Him through personal prayer, through the reading of the Scriptures, and through living our lives fully in the Church. Once we understand the family as a domestic church we see that we never have to leave church again.

We can have faith because there is a God who loves us, who came among us, who died for us, who paid the price for our sin on Calvary, who was raised from the dead, who ascended, who poured out His Spirit, who established the Church, and who continues to lead us and guide us. We can have faith in that fact, and we should teach our children to have faith in that fact, make it their own, and make Him their own.

The goal in the rearing of our children, fathers and mothers, should be to produce saints for the Lord and the Church. That's right, saints—those consecrated and set aside for the Lord. Perhaps some of our children will actually become canonized saints, but all of our children, by virtue of their baptism have been claimed and set aside by God. We need to help them live their call of sainthood, embrace the promise of their baptism, and live a life worthy of their calling (Col. 1:10).

If we are to teach our children these truths, we need to believe them ourselves. We are called to teach our children to believe in God who is Father, Son, and Spirit; to believe in God's revelation as taught to us through the Scriptures; to believe in God's personal providence, in His love for each person. Jesus told us that there is not a hair on our head that is not numbered, and not one sparrow falls to the ground without His knowing (Luke 12:7). That is the kind of love God has for us. We need to have faith in that love, experiential faith, evangelical faith rooted in its source, the Evangel, Jesus Christ.

Are we living lives of faith in the home? Are we acting on faith, or are we acting on fear or circumstances? How do we approach difficulties, struggles, travail, and trial? The way we treat those kinds of realities in our daily home life is the way our children will treat them because they imitate us and follow our example.

To exemplify and demonstrate faith in the home, we should look at some basics. How do we approach financial pressure and unemployment, difficult periods of life, struggles, sickness? With faith? Sickness in the family seems to be particularly difficult, but we have to realize that our bodies are corruptible. Yes, we believe in healing, and we ought to pray as a family for healing, but at the same time we need to realize that final healing comes in the resurrection of the body. Sickness and suffering are facts of life. We approach them in faith or they will destroy our faith.

The primary reason that we teach our families to believe is because it is necessary for salvation (Rom. 10:9), but faith is also one of the essential elements of living a vibrant Christian life, in the whole Church and in the domestic church. In the early church, the Scripture tells us, "All that believed were together" (Acts 2:44). Their belief was the foundation of their ability to live out the command of Jesus Christ and to carry out His mission.

So it is in our life as family. We need to believe in God's providence. We need to have faith, faith that will not quit when things get difficult, faith in good times and bad. We need to live it and teach it to our children. That is the kind of faith that the Christian family needs in these days, the kind of faith that will move mountains, change situations, and bring hope to a troubled world. Revival for the whole Church must begin behind the front doors of its smallest cell, the family.

Faithfulness to God in the family also makes our church experience richer because church is primarily about community; church is a family of families. When we can respond to God in faith within the domestic church, we can better understand our communal mission as the entire Body of Christ. For this reason, our ministry as domestic church is strengthened. We become more what we are supposed to be, light and leaven for our children and, as a family, for the world and the Church universal. If you want to change the church and the world, change your family.

Belief in God and faith in His promises should be taught and initiated, developed and interpreted, defined and encouraged, appropriated and lived out. All of these things happen in the day-to-day circumstances and situations of our lives together as "church in miniature."

We, the domestic church, can be witnesses and examples to the whole Church, and indeed to the world, that a mustard seed of faith can move mountains and change lives. That is the faith of our fathers, the faith of our Church, the faith that Jesus Christ desires His people to have. That is the faith that our families can have, mothers and fathers, children together, the domestic church living by faith in the Lord.

12

The Domestic Church at Work

It was the first cool day of autumn in Virginia. It was also a Saturday. We gathered the troops around the kitchen table for breakfast and announced the plans for the day. We were all going to rake leaves. You would have thought we had dropped the atom bomb. The frowns stretched to the floor and the sighs were as loud as the wind howling outside the window. "But Dad, it's Saturday," came the response from the children. After much resistance, we stationed all the children within arm's length in an assigned area. We all began the task.

I had the back yard with my son Keith (who frowned and sighed the hardest) and my daughter Ann (who was his runner-up). It took about an hour, but before long the work became a vehicle for family time, instruction, and enjoyment. As we filled the bags we jumped in the leaves, and we talked about what was most important to each of our hearts. By the end of the day we were tired in a good way, the way only hard work can make you tired. We had accomplished a task that needed to be accomplished, and we had drawn closer, experiencing the unity so necessary for a family truly to be a domestic church.

All of this through work? That's right. Because contrary to how our children first reacted, work (that all too often avoided reality) can become the vehicle for our own change. It is also a way in which we can reflect the very nature of God, individually and as a family.

Again, John Paul echoes centuries of Christian teaching on work:

Man is made to be in the visible universe in the image and likeness of God Himself, and he is placed in it in order to subdue the earth. From the beginning therefore he is called to work. Work is one of the characteristics that distinguish man from the rest of creatures, whose activities for sustaining their lives cannot be called work. Only man is capable of work, and only man works, at the same time by work occupying his existence on earth."[1]

Jesus reminds us in the Gospel of John of the heart of all Christian work: "This is the work of God, that you believe in the one he sent" (John 6:29).

The domestic church is a working church. Work is at the heart of its mission. Just as work is at the heart of the mission of the universal church. The work of the Church is evangelization, sanctification, and transformation. Evangelization of the world (and re-evangelization of its members), sanctification of itself and all who will come into its midst through the doorway who is Jesus Christ, and transformation of the temporal order. It is the work of the Church to believe in what Jesus said and to do what Jesus did. It is the work of the domestic church to do the same.

Perhaps more than any other place, this whole area of work is riddled with confusion in the minds of most contemporary Christians and, for that matter, most secular people. To many Christians, work is problematic. On the one extreme, Christians can be the worst workaholics, transferring our cultural obsession with performance and function into a misguided notion of frantic ministry. That is why the preceding chapter on leisure came first in this book.

At the other extreme there are those who see work as a part of the curse and a fruit of sin. This is also woefully mistaken.

Adam and Eve were given their work assignments from the Lord prior to the fall (Gen. 1:28–30). After the Fall the fruit of their sin was useless toil. Christian work is not useless toil. As those who follow in the footsteps of Jesus, our work is the most useful of all because it is joined to the work of the one who said, "My food is to do the will of the one who sent me and to finish his work. Do you not say, 'In four months more the harvest will be here'? I tell you, look up and see the fields ripe for the harvest" (John 4:34).

God is at work even to this day accomplishing His purposes through Christ and through those who belong to Christ. From the beginning (which is what the word *genesis* means) God was at work. And He called those whom He fashioned in His image to work. That call was codified for His chosen people in the Ten Commandments. "Six days you may labor and do all your work. . . . You shall not steal. . . . You shall not covet your neighbor's house. . . . his ox or ass, nor anything else that belongs to him" (Exod. 20:9, 15, 17).

The leaders of the Jewish people, their rabbis, did not accept money for teaching, but earned their money at crafts. It is out of this lineage that Paul the apostle, the tentmaker, came.[2] This Jewish understanding of work grew from the Old Testament revelation that, in fact, in working man was reflecting the image of his Creator. It was also quite contrary to the thinking of the contemporary pagan world.

The Greeks called work "ponos" which actually meant "punishment." Those who labored the hardest were considered the lowest in society. This also is a consistent theme in Aristotle and Plato. This certainly is not the Christian view of work.[3]

When Jesus was harassed for healing the man at the pool He spoke to His accusers and told them, "My Father is at work until now, so I am at work" (John 5:17). Work is a blessing, not a curse. Obviously we need to look at work in a new way if we are going to understand it as a blessing.

God worked to create the world, and He continues to work through us to transform His creation. He is at work sanctifying, redeeming, and transforming the world through those who follow in the footsteps of His Son. Christian parents need to both demonstrate and impart this concept to their children. We desperately need a renewed sense of work in this age.

As was demonstrated in the story at the beginning of this chapter, all work within the domestic church can produce tremendous fruit. It unifies. There is nothing like working together on a task outside of ourselves that enables a family to draw together. It promotes a sense of self-worth, dignity, and purpose. How often have we realized that when the work we dreaded the most was accomplished well, it brought us a great sense of pride.

Work can also be sanctifying insofar as it changes and transforms our character. Often it is through the discipline of work that we learn to be docile, rightly obedient, and committed to an end. It is creative in that it often literally transforms the physical environment. Of course a simple example is our own yard which, on that fall day, desperately needed to be transformed. By the end of the day it was beautiful to Laurine and me. (Of course our kids thought it was beautiful when the leaves were on the ground. Beauty truly is in the eye of the beholder.)

Finally work provides the opportunity for parents to impart practical and spiritual principles to the children and for brothers and sisters to be peer models and teachers to one another.

In the biblical mandate to "subdue the earth" men and women are given a very holy and privileged position in the order of things. They are called to be cocreative. They are called to be agents of the creator. They are also called to transform their society. In a very real sense work goes far beyond the back yard. The call to Christian work must propel Christian people into the marketplace, the courtrooms, the legislatures, the schools, and the mills. Through creating an environment wherein work is dignified for what it truly is, we will present our children to the world as Christian adults ready to carry on the work of God.

However, we all too often fall prey to the temptation to compartmentalize our life. This is most true in many contemporary Christian circles. We hear in those circles about areas that are somehow "spiritual" or "religious" (such as prayer, praise, ministry) and others that are not (such as work, recreation, or so called "secular" pursuits). If we really understand the Incarnation, however, God did not become flesh for just those religious occasions of our life. In fact, by becoming flesh, God transformed the whole of our lives, made it holy and restored it to its original dignity. For the Christian, the Incarnation means that the whole of human experience is impregnated with the very life of the Spirit of God. There is no spiritual or secular dichotomy. God did not make a distinction between holy and non-holy actions in the six days of creation. Each of the activities He engaged in was holy because He was doing it, and so it is with us. Similarly everything His Son did during His earthly ministry was holy. He lives within us and we are indeed temples of the Holy Spirit (1 Cor. 3:16). Though it may sound odd, when we go to work He goes with us because He dwells within us.

Jesus was and is at work. During His earthly ministry He was a carpenter, and His human foster father, Joseph, was a working man. Those who followed in Jesus' footsteps, like the apostle Paul, were working men and women. Paul was probably a tentmaker (Acts 20:34–35). He so understood the importance of work that he chastised those who were "living in idleness . . . not doing any work" (2 Thess. 3:11 RSV). He went on to instruct the community of Thessalonica that if anyone would not work he was not to eat (2 Thess. 3:10). This was not mean-spirited, but rooted in a deep understanding of the importance of individual responsibility and the dignity of work.

Among numerous passages in the New Testament on work, perhaps the admonition to the Colossian Christians is most instructive "whatever you do, work at it with all your heart, as working for the Lord, not for men, since you know that you will receive an inheritance from the Lord as a reward. It is the Lord Christ you are serving" (Col. 3:23–24). Herein lies the true dignity of the Christian's work. Whether washing clothes, mopping a floor, changing diapers, pouring molten steel in a steel mill, or arguing in a court of law, she or he is no longer doing it simply for self, but for the Lord. This is true for everyone of us and for each of our children.

It is up to us to rescue the Christian work ethic for an age when it is desperately needed. This is one of the challenges to the domestic church of the family—to bring about a renewal of a Christian understanding of work at this critical time in history. In our own nation, the American work ethic is at an all-time low.[4] We have witnessed the collapse of a communist system in Europe that divorced work and the human experience from God's laws and love. We are now witnessing the Church losing its Incarnational worldview and being relegated to a Sunday experience. As a result, Christians have abandoned many important responsibilities in the temporal world. Yet we are called to renew the temporal order through work, through political and social involvement, through taking personal and societal responsibility, and through prayer. This understanding of Christian mission will only be restored if we take up the banner under the roof of our own homes.

The domestic church at work is the family centered in Christ, understanding that everything it engages in flows out of that central conviction in a profound and mysterious way and has eternal consequences and value. Of course the proclamation of the gospel is the primary goal of the Church as it is of the domestic church. But the demonstration of gospel values in the marketplace is the most powerful way most of us can assist in God's creative, redemptive, and sanctifying efforts on behalf of all the world. For God still loves the world so much that He gives His only Son through you and me.

13

The Domestic Church at Play

It was a beautiful sunny day, one of those legal holidays that bank tellers, government workers, and school children take off, but most of us don't. As I prepared to leave for work, my two youngest children (the only ones awake yet) came to hug me goodbye. MaryEllen's joyful little eyes looked up into mine, and she said, "Dad, can't you stay home and play with us today?" "Yeah, Dad," said Joel, "Can't you watch the Flintstones?"

What could I say? I smiled, told them to have a wonderful day, and prayed a blessing over them. But for the rest of the day I mulled over what they had said. At a noon prayer meeting I attended, Pat Robertson delivered a message that hit me again. He referred to Mark 2:27–28: "The sabbath was made for man, not man for the sabbath. That is why the Son of Man is lord even of the sabbath." It reminded me once again of my children's wish to have me stay and play with them.

Satan is often referred to in Scripture as "Beelzebub," or "lord of the flies." But this name can also be translated "lord of frantic or useless activity." It makes sense, doesn't it? Flies buzz around from place to place. They seldom rest. Similarly we get involved in all kinds of unnecessary activity too. Our churches often reinforce this frantic feeling, as we go from meeting to meeting, rather than from glory to glory!

One of God's names in the Old Testament is Lord Sabaoth, or

"Lord of rest." And in the New Testament Jesus promised rest to the weary. So why are we so frantic? Are we really meeting our ultimate goals with all our hurry and bother? Does God take any pleasure in our rushing about to "serve" Him?

Irenaeus, one of the Latin fathers of the Church, once spoke a profound truth that is a fitting response to our question. He said, "The glory of God is man fully alive."[1] *To be fully alive*. What does that mean? I believe we shine more greatly as we continue to become the fullest persons that God has created us to be.

Becoming and being fully human is a notion that carries with it a certain amount of ambiguity. Many people never even address the question. For those who do, there exists a wide range of conscious and unconscious thoughts about what it means to be human. For example, many atheist thinkers have struggled with this notion of being human and have arrived at a self-sufficient humanity, one that can build, create, and be its best through the powers of reason or action.

This philosophy has quite a following. However, many philosophers radically disagree. Some may suggest God as a Prime Mover and humanity as created in His image and likeness, but they see God as having no further role. Still others may not affirm a need for human energy, but only God's power as the transforming agent for the human being. These are but a few examples of the foundations from which people begin to talk about being human.

Following the example of John Paul II, I fall somewhere in between the latter two. I believe that each person is created by God in His divine image and likeness and, therefore, to the extent that each creature becomes like God, he fulfills his potential. Many would say that this view limits each individual's uniqueness. If we are all to become like God, we'll all be carbon copies of each other. That would be true if God were human or if He were simply a one-dimensional Spirit. But if God is infinite beauty, truth, goodness, wisdom, and love, each of us will share His infinitude in an unique way. So will our children.

As much as our spirits cry out against conformity, our society reinforces that very value. We hold financial success as a gauge for personal success. Moreover certain clothes, cars, or other material goods give us a specific identity. As an attorney, I know there is a specific way to "be" in the courtroom. The color of the suit, the tie, the shoes, the mannerisms, and tone of voice are all externals that lawyers use to look a certain way. The same is true for employees of large corporations, conservative politicians, yuppies, and even those who seem to be unique, such as artists or actors. Even they have their rules; all must dress uniquely, conforming to the code of nonconformity.

As much as we desire individuality and want to nurture our uniqueness, there are attributes all humans share. All of us are created to love and be loved. All are created with a desire for community. All are created for union with God. Because of this, we can talk about certain perspectives on the Christian life, specifically Christian family life, without eliminating individual and unique personal responses to these general truths.

The personal, unique dimensions of every creature are God-given and should be developed in godly ways. A question that becomes increasingly significant for me, as a church member and father, is "Do we allow people the freedom to explore themselves, to grow emotionally, and to be comfortable in what God has created?" I realize that sounds a bit like the 1960s "I just wanna be me" mentality, but here is something profound.

Many of us, while we were growing up, carried the pressure of "becoming something." Did you ever hear or say, "I want to make something of myself when I grow up"? The unconscious pressure behind such a statement is phenomenal. The underlying value is that material success will lead to freedom—a very dangerous philosophy. But our temptation today is to create greater bondage by reducing men and women to function. I produce, therefore, I am. I can provide for myself, therefore, I am free.

This unhealthy value has led to extensive workaholism and a general devaluing of the need for relaxation and recreation. We never want to go to the other extreme and negate the value of contributing to society. Work, as we saw in the last chapter, is also integral to our human dignity. Neither extreme is healthy. Certainly human nature involves a development of skills and abilities and responsibility. Being human also involves personal relationships, an adherence to a set of values and belief systems, and many other things. But not one of these activities, nor even all of them put together, exhaust what it means to be human.

The Value of Play

Full human development involves something much deeper. The inner core of the self must attain a level of comfortability with just being, not doing. At this point, I want to discuss the concept of play. This may puzzle many of you. Isn't play something that we encourage the kids to do? How can play become a part of daily life for the entire family? That these questions even surface indicates an incomplete understanding of the human experience, one that involves mind, will, emotions, all integrated in some way.

Those who have written about play, leisure, and rest have difficulty defining it. Robert Johnston is helpful as a starting point. He suggests any "player is a changed individual because of the play time, his or her life having been enlarged beyond the workaday world."[2]

Part of being human is resting from work. It is inhuman not to rest, we might say that our society has trained us to be less than human. Clearly humans are meant to break from work. God gave us a model for resting in the story of Creation and even in the Gospels.

The book of Genesis tells us of the six days in which God created the world. We all know that He rested on the seventh day. But what we may not remember is that God rested each of those days. In fact, even the operation of Creation was very leisurely. God could have thought everything into instant being. Instead, however, day by day He created more of the painting, took time to enjoy each brush stroke, and then rested. The sabbath or seventh day, then, becomes the culmination of His leisure, a punctuation mark perhaps.

In the Gospels as well, Jesus often steps away for time to be alone, to regroup, to be with the Father (Matt. 14:13; Luke 14:35). Even the Lord needed time to rest from teaching, healing, preaching, and giving. His human body needed food, sleep, and rest. These times of rest for Jesus and for us today allow us to enter into communion with the divine.

Johnston suggests that the emphasis on communion with God was the foundation for the writer of the letter to the Hebrews. Unfortunately that union for which we were created has been marred by disobedience and we can no longer enter fully into God's rest or enjoy that perfect communion. Hebrews 4:11, 16 reads, "Therefore, let us strive to enter into that rest. . . . Let us confidently approach the throne of grace to receive mercy and to find grace for timely help." The writer seems to offer hope that what is incomplete now will one day be made complete, "the people of God entering fully into his rest."[3]

More Than Rest

This concept of leisure is critical to our understanding of the Christian life, especially of our purposes in Christian family life. But leisure is much more than resting. Leisure involves "being" and having the freedom to be. In our homes, do we give permission for family members to have time alone to relax, doing whatever helps them unwind? Do we as a family play together? Or, parents, do we make our kids work outside all day Saturday or do their homework immediately after school. Do we sap the leisure out of our family time together by talking business or making the kids talk about what they learned in school that day? Certainly there is a time for that conversation, but it is anything but relaxing. In fact, the opposite is true. When the focus remains business or school, the functionary soldier marches on.

Being together in the family is more than having a set time for meals or a service project or going to church or having family prayer. Somehow we need to integrate the recreative aspect of play into our family time. For my wife and I as a couple, play means something very different than with our children. We love to just spend time together, often not talking, not doing, just being.

The children, however, do not find being alone and quiet extremely recreative! They need something more concrete to do. Outings, movies, dinners out, or family games work well for us as long as we stress the personal encounter over the competition of a game. Competition is healthy in many ways, but not as a means of counteracting a spirit already flooded with a success mentality. The person-to-person time to share is what we find helpful.

Personal encounter doesn't necessarily have to happen on the outing or during the picnic. Often functional activities can serve the personal encounter. My son and I may be out raking leaves or trimming bushes, but these may be some of the greatest father/son moments we have. We can cooperate together in things that seem like work as long as the *encounter* takes precedence.

An Attitude

Leisure is all in the approach. As Joseph Pieper says in his book *Leisure: The Basis of Culture,* "Leisure is an attitude of heart."[4] The attitude for the Christian family is family-building. The first key to family-building is to have every member centering on God and leisure time with Him. Second we must learn to be present with and available to others, raising our relationships in the family above tasks and functions. A simple example of this would be helping clean up after a big meal. My temptation would be to wash the dishes myself because I can do it faster than some others in the family. In my frenzy to finish the task, I miss the joy of the encounter with family members who want to help.

Play or leisure is one need among many needs in the Christian family, and it must be so prioritized. I encourage you not to allow leisure to become another "job." It's easy to fall into an inappropriate attitude here, one that defeats the purpose. "Our family needs time to break from work. We'll take an hour every night after dinner and play together." So after dinner one of the kids runs at breakneck speed to get a game, sets up the board in a flurry of activity, and each player in turn rushes to roll the dice, spin the wheel, or move the piece so we can get as much of the game in as possible in one hour.

Freedom

It's all in the attitude. Play should produce peace, not tension. Leisure brings a sense of freedom, and this freedom allows us to increasingly grow as human beings. John Paul II teaches that to be a person is to be free. Paul in his letter to the Galatian Christians says, "For freedom Christ set us free" (Gal. 5:1). We were created and redeemed so that we could experience the fullness of life as totally free human beings. In the family, we want to help each other grow in greater and greater freedom. We do this by building up our members, by affirming their being, by helping them grow, and by possibly creating a space where the heart and soul can expand.

In my passion to see a full life of domestic church in our home, I have made many mistakes, and almost all of them have been in this area of freedom. For years Laurine and I were involved with a strong Christian group that eventually became legalistic. As a leader of the group, I didn't feel I could teach on anything I had not demonstrated in my own life. (That alone caused great bondage.) Consequently my home became a sort of laboratory for the group's teachings. At its most extreme, we almost became a family monastery of sorts. Our life was so structured that we squeezed the grace, spontaneity, and freedom of gospel living right out through the chimney. Later, by the grace of God, we saw that our rigidity was not helping the children. Also by the grace of God, we adjusted our life-style before it produced the almost inevitable fruit of legalism: rebellion.

I am convinced that very few groups set out to become legalistic. It is a subtle process that unfolds as one attempts to move from grace to compliance with the law. So it was with the Galatians. Paul reminded them to "stand firm and do not submit again to the yoke of slavery" (Gal. 5:1b).

One of the goals of Christian parenting is to help bring our children to a point of maturity in Christ wherein they freely choose to love and be loved. They freely choose to follow the law, but they do so out of love, not out of fear of punishment.

One example that most of us can relate to is the Von Trapp family in the much celebrated film *The Sound of Music*. As an ex-sea captain and a man badly hurt by the death of his wife, Captain Von Trapp enforced discipline and complete functionality in his children. They naturally rebelled (to everyone but their father). Not until the arrival of Maria did the children experience the freedom that accompanies affection, joy, love, play. She took them on picnics instead of obeying their father's direction to "march about the grounds breathing deeply." In response to the Captain's order to "drill them daily in their studies," she taught them about music, about fun, and about love. Maria brought with her the freedom of knowing how to enjoy life and live it to the fullest. Because of her influence, we see a family changed.

Maria (like her namesake Mary) was full of grace. That's what we need most: to be filled with God's grace. We need to be full of the unmerited favor and love that God freely bestows so that we can bestow it on our children. After all, they are His children first. It is part of His plan that they come into the full freedom of the sons and daughters of God. The gospel is all about freedom.

Freedom is also coming into a greater awareness of who we are, letting the mystery of who I am unfold. We cannot do this in a context of pure functionality because no creature of God is purely functional. Our very self rebels against the thought. So often today, people are tragically reduced to nothing more than a file card—"You are the sum total of these qualities that I see." The self screams *"No!"*

We are incredibly limited by others' perceptions of us, but the truth is that no one knows the whole me except God. Not even I have unfolded much of the mystery of myself. We need time to discover and explore and become comfortable with ourselves. In this way, as we identify and become settled with ourselves, we can embrace more of the human creation that God set in motion.

We will increasingly unfold into His likeness and thus experience the joy for which we were created.

14

In the World But Not of It

For me, one of the most powerful ways to experience God is to plant myself in the heart of nature, drinking in the luminous reality of God's creation. Francis of Assisi well knew the glory of God in the natural order. He purposely chose beautiful places to pray because for him, these were clear, expressive revelations of God. A good friend visited Assisi recently and shared a profound experience with me.

Francis and his brothers built a hermitage high in the mountains of Italy near Assisi. My friend visited this hermitage (called Il Carceri) with the intention of touring the few small buildings and having a short time of prayer in the stone chapel. She recounted being thankful she had gone alone because, as soon as she stepped foot into the confines of the hermitage and gazed on the valleys below, she knew she would be there for quite some time.

After exploring the few buildings on site, my friend was drawn to the surrounding woods where each brother had carved his own prayer cave in the rocks of the mountain. Her spirit soared as she made her way through the dirt paths of the hills. The leaves were drenched from the morning rainfall, and they dripped freely upon her head. But an abundance of sunshine also blazed through every crack it could find. Water and light mingled together, nature and grace, time and eternity, earth and heaven all at once. She told me she became engulfed in it all, powerless to escape had she even desired to.

She told me of having grasped at that instant a glimpse of what Mary must have felt as she sang, "My soul proclaims the greatness of the Lord" (Luke 1:46). Every impulse was ignited and all her energy was stimulated as she allowed the power of the Most High to overshadow her. For her, it was a true encounter with the divine, a visitation of God. But that is the potential of God's creation because everything about it has the stamp of the Almighty.

From the book of Genesis, we know that God created the world, and He saw that everything in it was *very good*. All of creation was hurled into motion by the hand of God, is marked by Him, and is therefore fundamentally good. There is so much to enjoy about the created world. I believe God loves much of our world—culture, art, music, poetry, dance, drama, good humor. These are creations of the human mind and imagination and, therefore, extensions of the creativity of God.

Take, for example, music. Music moves the soul. It has the ability to calm, excite, or stir up any number of healthy emotions. Similarly the power of music can lead to negative behavior and thinking so we need to always be careful of what our minds feed on.

I am convinced, however, that tapping into the creative part of our soul and feeling life with the depth of our emotions is one of the most human and life-giving actions of which we are capable. It can bring to life human creativity, the creative spirit within us and allow us in a powerful way to share in the creativity of God. God does not ask for a spartan environment devoid of rich creativity. In fact, these glorify Him in the richest way as they mirror His creative image. Think about it: When we sing, write, think, imagine, and love, what is the result? Music, poetry, ideas, images, and life. These are goods born of God Himself. We need to live these truths in our family. Life is a gift, Creation is a gift, and our life together is a gift. It should be accepted as holy.

The Crown of His Creation: You and Me

Similarly, but even more profoundly, should we reverence the hand of God in the pinnacle of His creation: man and woman, the only creatures of God made in his divine likeness: "Then God said: 'Let us make man in our image, after our likeness.' . . . God created man in his image; in the divine image he created him; male and female he created them" (Gen. 1:26–27).

The Scriptures also tell us, "God so loved the world that he gave his only Son" (John 3:16). *The world* in this sense refers to men and women, the most precious of His creations. God does love the world; He loves each man, each woman, each child, and wants to redeem us all.

We, too, are created to love each man, woman and child and thirst for their salvation. We long for relationship and fellowship and love because God made us that way. Loving and being loved stirs within us the deepest emotions and the greatest expression of life. To "love the world" in this sense is to fulfill our deepest desires, our God-given needs, and to enter the fullness of joy.

But neither the created order nor mankind is what we refer to as the negative definition of *the world*. The world that Christians are called to fight is the active, aggressive system of values, structures, and relations that are evil and opposed to God and His people. God no longer reigns in this system because people have chosen not to obey Him. All of us have certain unhealthy systems or patterns from which we work, and we need to identify, break, and root them out of our heart and family. We should plant in their place the values and systems of the kingdom of God. But there is also a system outside of ourselves and our homes that actively comes against God's order for our lives. In this sense, these worldly values are our enemy.

Jesus taught very clearly in His earthly ministry that there is a power at work in the world, and that power is sin. And the devil is the master of sin. Let us not be deluded. The Church has taught faithfully, and continues to teach faithfully, that "our struggle is not with flesh and blood but with the principalities, with the powers, with the world rulers of this present darkness, with the evil spirits in the heavens" (Eph. 6:12). We are dealing with a diabolical effort to undermine God's plan for family.

As sons and daughters of God, we are not subject to the world and do not need to succumb to that which is against God. We have been freed of its clutch on our families. The apostle Paul tells the Colossian Christians, "He delivered us from the power of darkness and transferred us to the kingdom of his beloved Son" (Col. 1:13). Paul is saying that we have been rescued from the world and have been brought into the kingdom.

In John's Gospel, Jesus says,

> But now I am coming to you. I speak this in the world so that they may share my joy completely. I gave them your word, and the world hated them, because they do not belong to the world any more than I belong to the world. I do not ask that you take them out of the world but that you keep them from the evil one. They do not belong to the world any more than I belong to the world. Consecrate them in the truth. You word is truth. As you sent me into the world, so I sent them into the world. And I consecrate myself for them, so that they also may be consecrated in truth. (John 17:13–19)

Throughout the New Testament we see that phrase *the world* coming back again and again. In the letter of James he says, "You adulterous people, don't you know that friendship with the world is hatred toward God? Anyone who chooses to be a friend of the world becomes an enemy of God" (James 4:4 NIV). The world in this sense is actually the enemy of God mainly because the world is ruled by Satan, the archenemy of the Lord, the Antichrist, the "ruler of this world" (John 12:31).

Since the enemy rules this world's system, it is a breeding ground for sin: "sensual lust, enticements for the eyes, a pretentious life . . . is from the world" (1 John 2:16). And as we all have experienced, each time we sin, we damage or choke the life of

God within us. Sin pulls us farther and farther from God until finally we fail to recognize sin, blocking our consciences and becoming immersed in a self-centered reality. Paul reminds us in 1 Corinthians 11:32 that there is judgment for those who live only in the world and that "the Lord chastens us to keep us free from being condemned with the rest of the world."

The Challenge We Face

While our attitude to the world must be clear, we must confront the challenge. The challenge is to cling to the good that is in the world, and fight to change the evil. We are not called out of the world; we are called to be in the world, to renew and change the world. Taking on the world is a huge and frightening risk.

Our temptation as Christian parents is to shield our children and ourselves from the world. We fear that the values we have worked so hard to instill in our children will become confused or infiltrated with secular values. That is a valid fear, but the fact remains: We are called to be in the world. The leaders of the Catholic church, in *Church in the Modern World,* remind all Christians of the role of the Church:

> The members of the earthly city are called to form the family of
> the children of God and to increase it continually until the Lord
> comes. . . . Thus the church, at once "a visible organization and a
> spiritual community," travels the same journey of all mankind. . . .
> It is to be leaven and, as it were, the soul of human society in its
> renewal by Christ.[1]

Though the reference here is specifically to the universal Church and its role in the modern world, as the church in miniature, the family likewise must become leaven in the world.

In John Paul's letter to the lay faithful of the church, he exhorts us to

> Keep a watchful eye on this our world, with its problems and
> values, its unrest and hopes, its defeats and triumphs: a world

whose economic social, political, and cultural affairs pose problems and grave difficulties. . . . This then is the vineyard; this is the field in which the faithful are called to fulfill their mission.[2]

Our call is to take our place in the world and for our families to make a difference. The challenge is to see our families as a sacred reality in the midst of a secular reality. Instead of becoming insular and retreating from the world, that vision can allow us to create an environment in which we don't avoid the world but rather provide for our children a stable, moral, holy foundation as a viable alternative to the values of the world.

Creating this environment is a continual process of daily choices and readjustments. There are no black and white answers to the difficult situations that arise in the family. For instance, one of my children may come home one day with a new friend. I'll call her Susie. As we learn more about this friend, we realize that the family system and values from which Susie comes are altogether different from what we want our children to learn. What does a parent do in this situation to be responsible without trying to control our children's entire lives? Laurine and I believe our children need to be exposed to people and values of the world at some point. If we shelter them all through their childhood, and they never learn how to deal with the world, they may later become infatuated with its values. So, in the situation with Susie, we don't forbid the two to spend time together, but we do suggest that Susie come to our house. In this way, we are more secure about their interaction. Also, Susie experiences our way of life and our values as well.

The point here is that we have come to believe that it is more dangerous and limiting to surround ourselves with one type of person.

My wife and I have come to this belief after some real mistakes. As I mentioned earlier, for a number of years we helped to build and lead and whole group of Christians who zealously followed the Lord, but gradually grew legalistic. In our early days we were a large weekly prayer meeting, but a core of us wanted to be more than that. We took the heart of the New Testament to be our own heart. We desired to live radically, to demonstrate to the world the truth of the gospel. For the first few years, we did so through fruitful evangelism. However, we then took a precarious detour on our way to the "deeper life." Without even realizing it, we began to withdraw from the world. We all began to move into the same neighborhoods, building our own "Christian culture" where our children would only be influenced by the "values of the kingdom." We tried to extract ourselves from all "worldly influences"—and that eventually included all non-Christians. That is not the Great Commission! It does not follow Jesus' example. And it does not produce the necessary fruit in the life of a Christian family: charity, love, and a Christlike passion for the people of the world.

Following the Master's Lead

Jesus would have never commanded us, nor would the Church teach so fervently to be in the world if that were not vital and possible. We are never placed in situations without the strength to combat and overcome them. God has given us all the tools we need to fight the world. But we need to use them. We need to use our faith, take risks, boldly live the truth in a world brimming with deception.

Jesus' life is the proof we have of the need to live in the world. What do we know about the life of Jesus? We know that He grew up in an orthodox Jewish home in the Galilee, nurtured by a mother and father who feared the Lord. He studied the Torah and learned the trade of His earthly father, spending time in His home and the temple. He grew up in a normal family. But of His public three years, we know that Jesus took to the streets. The fact is that He did not spend most of His time in the temple. Of course, He went to the temple to pray and teach, but His ministry was largely in the marketplace.

We know as well by the testimony of the scribes and pharisees that Jesus spent much of that time with the most unlikely people.

Three years He spent touching the untouchables: the lepers, sinners, women, Gentiles, all of whom the Jews avoided vehemently. Not only did He touch them and heal them, He spent time with them and broke bread with them. In the Jewish culture, this was a high sign of respect. Jesus elevated their humanity by treating them with dignity. He loved them, and in loving them, He lived out what He prayed to the Father for us: "I do not ask that you take them out of the world but that you keep them from the evil one" (John 17:15). Jesus embraced the world for the purpose of saving sinners. His love for the world threatened the world, but eventually overcame the world and ultimately will consume it.

Not only did Jesus *show* us how to be in the world, He also *taught* us. Particularly in the Sermon on the Mount, we learn the underlying values of the Christian life—humility, meekness, peace, purity, mercy. Further, immediately following the sermon in Matthew's Gospel, Jesus puts flesh to these values:

> You are the salt of the earth. But if salt loses its taste, with what can it be seasoned? It is no longer good for anything but to be thrown out and trampled underfoot. You are the light of the world. A city on a mountain cannot be hidden. Nor do they light a lamp and then put it under a bushel basket; it is set on a lampstand, where it gives light to all in the house. Just so, your light must shine before others, that they may see your good deeds and glorify your heavenly Father. (Matt. 5:13–16)

As disciples and as families, we are called to be salt and light for the world. In essence, what Jesus means by being salt and light is that, individually, we as Christians and Christian families are called to transform the world by our presence in it. Salt has many purposes, but I believe the key function as it relates to this passage is to enhance. The actual purpose of salt is not so much to give flavor, but rather to draw out and enhance the already-existing flavor. Christians are to be sprinkled throughout the world to bring out the goodness of it. We are to look at the goodness in people and in our world, and try to accentuate what is positive without denying the negative.

Similarly our calling to be light is a great responsibility. When light enters darkness, it makes a difference. Light removes the lonely, desolate, fearful, impenetrable experience of darkness. That is precisely the experience of much of the world—*darkness*. We are called to make a difference, to shatter the darkness with the blazing glory of God. We are not to just bring light (by preaching the Word or through social action); we are actually to *be* light. As we become like Jesus, the light of the world, we radiate a portion of His glory. The light of Christ shines from within us.

The point is to be Jesus for the world. All the good we do in the temporal order is a way of incarnating the love of Christ. Every neighborhood block party or service project or community gathering in which we participate brings Jesus' love to more of the world.

Michael Waldstein, an advocate for Communion and Liberation, an evangelical movement of lay people in the Catholic church, asserts:

> The presence of God's love in the flesh is the central truth around which everything in Christianity revolves. The universal light of God's love radiates from a particular point in history, from the flesh of Jesus. . . . [The] Christian faith is the affirmation of Christ's presence now. Christ is present here and now in mystery through his own body, which is the church. The church is in some way a prolongation of the Incarnation. She is the concrete instrument through which the presence of God's love touches one now.[3]

Witness to the World

Our witness in the world is so important. It cannot be overbearing, but neither can it be lifeless or powerless. What kind of witness are our families to others? Do our families change the world by their presence?

Some good questions to ask in trying to identify when we are living a worldly life, rather than living godly lives in the world are: Does Jesus rule in our home? Would He be comfortable here? In our dinner conversations, would Jesus be comfortable? In our entertainment, would Jesus be entertained?

In our approach to media and television, what do we allow to enter our minds and hearts and the minds of our children? Are our decisions dominated more by the world than by the kingdom? Or are they dominated by the values of the kingdom and the teachings of the Church? We as Christians have a choice. We can either be overcome by the world, or we can overcome the world through Jesus Christ.

Unfortunately many have been deluded. There are myriads of false spiritualities hovering about trying to "convert" our children; many are ripe for the harvest. As a teenager during the sixties and seventies, I know I was ripe for conversion, and there were other agendas that attempted to win me. Anti-Christian leaders with Marxist agendas and all types of liberation approaches attempted to woo me into submission. Thank God I was protected by the seed of faith planted in me as a child.

Many people's worldview, value structures, and general morality have lapsed into ambiguous, confusing, lukewarm, self-evaluated systems that open the door for deception to take root in the mind and heart. We are responsible as parents to train our children in the ways of the Lord. Happily, while children are vulnerable to deception, they are at the same time ripe for growth in the Lord. Children are ripe for conversion of any kind. It seems to be a matter of who reaches them first. As parents we have the advantage of their formative years. But so often we miss the opportunity. We need to protect and nurture our families' faith and a knowledge of the danger of worldly systems.

There are ways to overcome the negative impact of the world. We must protect ourselves in some ways, but escape is not the answer. One of our main safeguards against the world is having Christian fellowship. Jesus knew the critical importance of this, so He established the Church. For ongoing support, we can form real communities in our homes and join as a family with the faith community in our area.

Henri De Lubac, a twentieth-century French theologian warns against building a solitary Christianity that emphasizes personal growth between God and me as the sole focus. De Lubac reminds us that the Church does emphasize growth in the interior life, but while he sees the Church as on the one hand mystical, he also knows that the Church is visible in the world.[4] For the individual, then, this means that we need the body, we need our family. In turn the family needs the larger community of the local church. And specific communities need the universal Church. None of these bodies can healthily exist or pretend to fulfill the Christian mission if self-contained: "The man who separates himself from the community of brotherhood turns imperceptibly from God to worship himself."[5]

The early Christians understood this. In the midst of difficulties, they banded together. They lived a different life-style. No matter where they were scattered throughout the world, they lived a different life-style, and others noticed. They understood that the call of the Master affected every area of their lives. Because they were Christians, and because they were marked by the cross, they were to approach all things differently from those who were not Christians. Their relationships with one another, their relationship with people who did not believe, the way they approached their work, the way they treated property, the way they handled dealing with the marketplace, the way in which they responded to struggle, the way in which they loved—all of these things were to came under the rule of God.

The same is true for us today. Our primary witness as families is the example of our life-style and we are to be different. Augustine said, "The Church is the world, reconciled."[6] The Church, in other words, is a permanent witness of what the world can be. People watch us. They watch how we react to stress, job pressure, financial struggles, health problems, and current events. For instance, as I wrote this chapter, my country was headlong in the midst of the Persian Gulf crisis. How do we as Christians respond to issues like that? Do we pray for peace, or do we hope the U.S. military will flex its muscles and prove to the world how powerful we are? Another political issue involves voting. Do we as responsible voters examine and discuss the issues and the platforms of the candidates? Do we know our candidate's stand on human life issues? Do we vote according to the values of the Church?

In other areas of life, do we work hard? Do we play hard? Do we celebrate the Christian holy days with fervor? These are the things that make us visible, indeed blazing beacons for the world, but at the same time protect us as we practice, own, and reinforce our values. When we all live by the same standards, not as clones but as people in common, then we become community.

Being part of the Church frees us from being trapped by the negative forces in the world. De Lubac in his book *The Splendour of the Church,* quotes Augustine's analysis of our situation in the following words:

> Man will, in this life, form part of two cities. . . . He will not stop being a member of an earthly city; but he will not be bound to the earthly city any more by the same exclusive ties as before, for he will have been given entry to a new city in which his new existence is to unfold. This new city . . . is the church. . . . It is through her that God recreates and re-forms the human race.[7]

Not of It

I remember reading the story of a cloistered contemplative monk, Thomas Merton, who once said something like this: "I did not rid myself of the world by going into a cell, because I took the world with me." We carry worldly values around, and that is what conversion is all about, making us holy like the Master we serve. Becoming holy, set apart for God—becoming like Jesus—is our goal. The heart of the mission of the domestic church is the sanctification of its members. The key for us as parents is to understand that we need to be free, and our homes need to be free from the negative pressures of the world and free also to enjoy the positive elements of the world. In the world, but not of it.

But being *in* the world does not mean being *like* the world. One danger is to become like them to win them. Many Christians in an attempt to "be real" or part of "the real world" compromise eternal values and truths for secular ones. A worldly mentality is not what the Lord asks for. When the apostle Paul directs us to be all things to all men (1 Cor. 9:19–20), he does not mean for us to confuse our values or change our standards. Rather, he realized the value in unconditionally meeting people where they are, not placing on others values that are beyond their scope of experience. For instance, we can't preach the Sermon on the Mount to friends who have never committed their lives to the Lord. Father George Montague, Scripture scholar, contends that the Sermon on the Mount was preached not to the crowds, but to those who dared to stand with Christ. We need to be sensitive to the world, to human beings in the world. How does one say, "Blessed are the poor in spirit, for theirs is the kingdom of heaven" (Matt. 5:3) to the CEO of a corporation, who is in love with material goods? We first need to introduce him to true riches, the "pearl of great price" (Matt. 13:46), who is Jesus Christ. Then the transformation can begin from the inside out.

How do we help our families live in the world without being of the world? Two key remedies to combat the world are transformation of mind and formation of community, both of which need to happen within our family units. Paul tells us throughout his letters (Rom. 12:2, Eph. 4:17) that our minds must be transformed to the mind of God. Then will we be able to judge what is truth and live holy lives pleasing to God.

How can we teach our families to have the mind of God? Mainly we can teach them to be rooted in the Scriptures. We need to teach our children that the Scriptures are the words that God wants us to know and live. His mind, his truth is recorded in the Bible. We need to provide for our children good teaching based on the Scriptures as well as the teachings of the Church.

For our family, as Catholic Christians, we believe the sacramental life is for transformation, particularly the Sacraments of

Reconciliation and the Eucharist. For all Christians, however, full participation of their whole family in church life will help them become more like Christ. We become more like Jesus each time we humbly confess sin and receive life-changing grace, and each time we receive God's Word through Bible reading or a sermon, or when we receive Jesus in the mystery of the Lord's Supper. In the full life of the Church, we are transformed continually, I believe, from glory to glory. We are to live in the Church in the midst of the world.

Sometimes as parents, I think we make a critical mistake. We act as though there is a moral vacuum outside of our homes, and so we often fail to recognize the competing agendas rivaling to win the hearts and minds of our children. If we do not impart the teaching of the Church, the teaching of the Scripture, the deposit of faith to them, who will? What will win the battle for their loyalties?

Let us not fall prey to the lie that tells us not to try to influence our children for God. We need to build a context, a culture, a way of life in our home where God is honored, and where the kingdom, the reign, the rule of God are established. To do this, we can rejoice in the realization that as the sacred Scripture teaches, "For the one who is in you is greater than the one who is in the world" (1 John 4:4). Greater is He that is in our home and in our marriage than he that is in the world.

The Rescue Mission

The Church at large and in miniature is on a rescue mission. Catholic leaders refer to the Church as the "seed of the kingdom," a seed that makes the kingdom present in the midst of the world, a seed that is constantly growing. I believe that's a wonderful image for us all. The domestic church is a seed of the kingdom, a place where the kingdom is manifested.

Jesus' earthly family is the model for all Christian families. In that family, Jesus was raised in the teaching of the Scriptures, taught a trade, and grew in wisdom and stature, we are told. Jesus was fully human *and* fully divine. Obviously His divinity did not need to increase. But in a very wonderful expression of love, God took on flesh and in His humanity allowed the tutelage of a human family to influence His human maturation. And as a family, they model for us the domestic church. The domestic church has Christ in its midst and brings Him forth for the world. That is why in many Christian traditions they are rightly called "the Holy Family."

The Holy Family experienced fellowship. They experienced God's solution to a world so troubled with difficulty, isolation, alienation, loneliness, despair and despondency. God's solution is the Church, and we are a part of it. They were our prototype. Under our roofs, we are called to live out what the full Church is, the seed of the kingdom of God, a place where God is manifested and the love of God is demonstrated, a place where children from an early age experience life in Christ.

We can and we *will* overcome the world. We will make our homes domestic churches if we are faithful to the charge we have as parents, and if we are faithful to the commission the Church is issuing in these days. Our home should be community, a place where believers—husbands, wives, and children—live together for the Lord and learn to serve one another, a place that reflects the whole church, a place of comfort and refuge for God's people. That is what we can become.

We need to be realistic. We also need to recognize that often we allow too much of the world into our homes and hearts. That is why Jesus prayed, "Holy Father, keep them in your name that you have given me" (John 17:11b). We, who are Christians by virtue of our baptism and our saying yes to Christ throughout our life, have made the choice to live for Christ. If we are serious about our families being the domestic church, we need to be serious about rooting the world out of our homes. We also need to understand that we have been placed in the world to carry on the mission of Jesus Christ, to transform the world. The answer to a needy world is the Lord who carries on His rescue mission through His people, the Church, and in a special way through its smallest and most intimate component, the domestic church.

15

Families on Mission

Throughout this book, we have sought a renewed understanding of family and of church and how these two realities coexist. The final step in the journey is to renew our understanding of our commission as the domestic church.

The mission of the Church is clear. Jesus commanded the disciples to go into the whole world and preach the gospel to every nation (Mark 16:15). The Church exists to evangelize. The Church strives to multiply itself, penetrate, and change the world. If the family is to become a miniature church, it must do what the Church does. Missionary work is required of the larger Church and, therefore, of its smaller segments, including the domestic church. We need to understand that evangelization is an integral part of Christian family living.

As the domestic church, we need to understand that we are missionary; this is not optional. Pope Paul VI, in *Evangelization in the Modern World*, reminded us all that the person who has been evangelized goes on to evangelize others: "Here lies the truth of evangelization. It is unthinkable that a person should accept the Word and give himself to the kingdom without, in turn, becoming a person who proclaims and bears witness to it."[1]

Do we bear witness to God in our neighborhood? Have others changed because of our example? Have they even noticed our example? The place of the Church in the twenty-first century depends on the family. The family plays such a vital role in the transformation of our world that we can truly say with John Paul II that "the path to the future passes through the family."[2]

What Is Mission?

The call to be missionary involves evangelization. Unfortunately the term *evangelism* threatens many Christians. Some would rather leave that task to "those who have the gifts." Certainly all are not called to be preachers or teachers, but all are called to evangelize in some way. Evangelization is simply sharing the good news that we have experienced since the moment of baptism, namely the forgiveness of sin and hope of eternal glory. The Church relies on her members to bring men and women into a saving relationship with Jesus Christ and into the family of the Church. Each person must discern his or her role within that charge, but for most Christian families, the call is to evangelize from the home and within the home through word and example.

We will see the fruit of mission within the home and in the neighborhood. Again, Paul VI speaks of the family mission: "The parents not only communicate the gospel to their children, but from their children they can themselves receive the same gospel as deeply lived by them." I know the truth of that. I know that I receive the good news from my children. It is such a blessing when they tell me what Jesus has done for them, or when they share an insight into the Scriptures.

My son Keith has particularly keen insight into Scripture sometimes. When he was nine, he shared such an insight with me concerning the vine and the branches passage (John 15). He said, "Jesus is the socket, isn't he? Jesus is the wall socket and we are the plug. We need to be plugged into Him for the power to live His life." We had just refinished our basement, and he was now familiar with wires, sockets, and electricity. That practical experience linked the Scripture to his heart to explain a very profound truth to both of us. We do need the power of the Spirit.

Without plugging into the socket, we could not possibly live this vision of the domestic church.

Paul VI also wrote,

> Such a family becomes the evangelizer of other families and of the neighborhood of which it forms part. We have been given all of this goodness not just for ourselves but to share it, to share it with our neighbors and coworkers and to do it as a family.

This kind of "family evangelization" happens in a very natural way. For example, when our relatives come to visit, we do not change our habits. In the early days of our marriage and childrearing, Laurine and I felt somewhat awkward continuing some of the spiritual disciplines we practiced when others stayed with us. We didn't want to "offend them." At the time, those habits included a much more formal morning and evening prayer session than they currently do. However, we decided it was more important to continue our devotions and invite our guests into them. And we gained wonderful results.

Similarly we continue to practice blessing our meals and saying bedtime blessings and prayers when our children have friends over. Once again, although it sometimes feels awkward, we have found that those who visit our home usually leave with a positive impression of Christianity.

I think we are too often ashamed of the gospel. We need to remember Romans 1:16: "I am not ashamed of the gospel. It is the power of God for the salvation of everyone who believes: for Jew first, and then Greek." The choice is ours.

The Early Church

This concept of family on mission is nothing new but is as old as the gospel itself. I always find it helpful to examine the life of the first Christians to see how they worshiped, how they learned, how they lived together. For the most part, the early church had no buildings, so it usually met for worship and instruction in homes, often centering around one family. These families were responsible for not only knowing the teachings, but also for modeling the Christian life. Considering the newness of the faith, these families obviously undertook tremendous responsibility and risk.

We know from history and tradition that Priscilla and Aquila offered their family's home to the church (Col. 4:15 NIV). They were primarily responsible for a church that met in their home, but their family also went on mission with Paul. Paul sent his greetings from Rome to Priscilla and Aquila, calling them his "fellow workers in Christ Jesus." He says, "They risked their lives for me. Not only I but all the churches of the Gentiles are grateful to them" (Rom. 16:3–4 NIV). They must have made a significant contribution to the development of the Church. How did they do this? From within their home. They did journey with Paul at times, but their primary mission was out of the home.

Faithful families like these allowed for the growth of the Church: "And every day the Lord added to their number those who were being saved" (Acts 2:47). Through dedicated, courageous families like Priscilla and Aquila, the gospel spread. God brought people to them and they shared the gospel. Many who heard believed and received God as Father, Jesus Christ as Savior and Lord, and the empowerment of the Holy Spirit. The Church expanded. The mission continued and we are here today professing the name "Christian" because of those early believers and their zeal for evangelization.

From the early church, we can see that we don't need to go to foreign lands to be missionary. That's impractical, not to mention a misunderstanding of the call. Certainly some are called to travel and preach to those who have never heard the name of Jesus. Obviously Paul and the apostles are the prime examples. But most people in the early church (and the modern church) lived out the call within the family. From families, they shared their faith. They understood that to be called by Christ as a family is to become missionary.

There is a beautiful reading from John Chrysostom on evangelization taken from a homily he preached on the missionary activity of the early church as recorded in the Acts of the Apostles:

> There is nothing colder than a Christian who does not seek to save others. You cannot plead poverty here, the widow putting in her two small coins will be your accuser. Paul was so poor that he was often hungry and went without necessary food. You cannot plead humble birth, for they were humbly born of humble stock. You cannot offer the excuse of lack of education, they were uneducated. You cannot plead ill health for Timothy had poor health with frequent illness. Each one can help his neighbor if only he is willing to do what is in his power. . . . Do not say it's impossible for me to influence others. If you are a Christian, it is impossible for this not to happen. Things found in nature cannot be denied. So here, for it is a question of the nature of a Christian. Do not insult God. If you say the sun can't shine, you've insulted Him. If you say a Christian can't help others, you've insulted God and called Him a liar. It's easier for the sun not to give warmth or shine than for a Christian not to shed his light. Easier for the light to be darkness than for this to happen. Do not say then that it is impossible, the opposite is impossible. If we have put our affairs in order these things will certainly come to be and follow as a natural consequence. The light of the Christian cannot escape notice, so bright a lamp can never be hidden.[3]

By virtue of our new nature (which we were given as a gift in baptism and which we reaffirm, cherish, nourish, and mature in our life in the Church) we are called to let our light shine, to be evangelizers as families and to share the good news.

John Paul II stated during his tour to the United States in 1987, "The family is the first setting of evangelization, the place where the Good News of Christ is first received, and then, in simple yet profound ways, handed on from generation to generation."[4] He ought to know; he was raised in a devoutly Christian family under the tyranny of an atheistic government. But he stands in a line of good fruit from good homes. In the holiness tradition, we have only to look to Susannah Wesley and her children. Christian offspring become Christian adults who hand on the gospel.

Knowledge and Action

This is the mindset we need to nurture. We cannot expect our children to learn the faith outside of our influence as parents. We cannot expect our family to be effective as a domestic church if we don't struggle to develop as one. We learn the gospel first in our homes. Then we share it within our homes. In turn, our families, strong in faith by building each other up, can corporately share Christ. This is a new way of understanding the mission of family, and as important as this new understanding is, we need even more. We need to take action, breathe life into our theory.

Knowledge is not enough. At some point, we are responsible for acting on that knowledge. In John's Gospel, after Jesus arose from the table at the last supper, He said, "I have set you an example that you should do as I have done for you. . . Now that you *know* these things, you will be blessed if you *do* them" (John 13:15, 17, emphasis added).

In the home, evangelization begins first as husbands share their faith and the truth of who Jesus is and the teachings of the Church with their wives and the wives with their husbands, parents with their children, brothers and sisters building one another up in the faith. The mission extends beyond the immediate family to include relatives, cousins, grandparents, neighbors, and co-workers. That is how, in the natural day-to-day events of our life, our faith reaches out to change hearts and lives.

The witness of our consecrated home, our daily life in Christ, and our love for one another are all powerful evangelistic tools. We should not underestimate the impact our example can have. People notice our behavior even in the mundane actions that we consider unspectacular. It's amazing what neighbors pay attention to. For instance, people see how we treat the mailman or the plumber, how we deal with hardship, and how we serve others in their hardship. These can be ways of expressing love for God and neighbor and are tremendous possibilities for evangelism.

Within all of these moments, do we see others as human beings in pain and in need of love? Or do we perhaps as overzealous number-seekers see them as another evangelistic challenge? Sensitivity is critical in any service for the Lord. Are we compassionate enough as families to recognize need and to reach out and meet it? Are we sensitive enough to use these occasions for conveying God's love? Are we sensitive enough to know when preaching is completely inappropriate? The way we approach people communicates much of how we think about mission.

My Own Family

Some of the most wonderful evangelistic encounters we have had as a family have been those occasions when we have been able to open our home to provide hospitality to good friends, community members, or someone in need. We share our everyday lives with our guests, morning and evening prayer, grace before meals and after meals, reflection on the sacred Scripture, relaxation, our normal lives. What is natural for us becomes natural for our guests. As they participate with us, the Lord is able to move in their lives, and the effect is evangelistic. We are trying to maintain a culture in our home, a culture that clearly says, "I am a Christian and I believe in Jesus Christ and I love my church."

We Christian families always have the goal of outreach before us, particularly in our immediate residential areas. We need to extend ourselves beyond the four walls of our home, remembering that we have been planted in our neighborhood for a purpose. There seems to be a contemporary phenomenon of closing out the rest of the world. How many people come home from work, push the garage door opener, drive in, shut the door behind them, and go into the house? I do quite frequently. But we must fight the temptation to make it the norm. God loves the rest of the world and gave His only Son for them. We need to love that world with the love of Christ. In a very real sense, the world is waiting for *our* family.

> At different moments of the church's history and the Second Vatican Council, the family has well deserved the beautiful name of Domestic Church. This means that there should be found in every Christian family the various aspects of the entire church. Furthermore, the family should be a place where the gospel is transmitted and from which the gospel radiates. In the family, conscious of this mission, all the family members evangelize and are evangelized.[5]

There are two accounts in the Acts of the Apostles that are particularly enlightening in this regard. In Acts 10, while Peter preaches, the Holy Spirit falls on Cornelius's whole household. That household, that family, became a source of strength and power for the mission of the early church.

In Acts 16, Paul and Silas were in prison, and the angel of God broke their chains. The jailkeeper became frightened. Paul and Silas preached the gospel and led the jailkeeper to conversion, and he and his entire household were baptized. The story continues that the jailkeeper and his family fed the apostles and took care of them.

In our own lives we have seen people change as they witness Christian family living. Truth is magnetic. In our work in Steubenville, we saw many families touched and changed by what they see in our church community's commitment to one another. Not long ago a devout, professional man decided to live more clearly for the Lord because of the witness of strong Catholic families that he met in Steubenville. He said, "I want that for my family." He went home and instituted family prayer, and it literally began to transform his family. So much so that he wrote to give praise to God for the change in every member.

There are so many people like him in the world, waiting for God to touch them through us. We all have circumstances in our lives where we can become ambassadors for Christ. We need to open our eyes to see them, and then take the opportunity. How many people come through our front doors? How many people come into our offices? How many people comment on how we take our faith seriously? Let us take these opportunities to tell them about our God.

I know my wife, Laurine, was won to faith in Christ and into the Catholic church through the simple witness of evangelistic Catholic friends. She began to ask questions and they were not afraid to share their faith. They were engaged in a personal evangelism. Personal evangelization simply means sharing the good news in the context of our daily life. We do not have to be eloquent or learned. We simply have to be who we are in Christ.

For the Christian family, this means openly expressing our faith in Jesus Christ. We can do this with one another in very natural ways. When a family member is sick it should naturally be the case that another member offers to pray and lay hands upon the sick one. Additionally when a family feels down, another member should naturally seek to encourage and lift up him or her, perhaps sharing a word from Scripture. Far from being unrealistic this kind of practical Christianity works and produces marvelous fruit.

My wife often shares a story of when she was a little girl. She was not raised in a particularly religious home, but her family regularly visited a particular neighbor, who was a Catholic Christian. When the neighbor family set up their Christmas tree, they prayed an ancient blessing acknowledging God and setting aside the tree to reflect the light of the gospel. That prayer had such an impact on Laurine that it still intrigued her as she went through her turbulent twenties. God was able to hook that interest and crack open the door of her heart.

Word and Life

But we need to share who we are both by our life-style and by our words. Sometimes we ask ourselves if demonstration of life isn't more important? Doesn't the way we treat others speak loudly to them? In many cases witness of life is the more appropriate response, but there are definitely circumstances that warrant the spoken word. Paul VI asserted that,

> The Good News that is proclaimed by the life is sooner or later proclaimed by the word of life. There is no true evangelization if the name, the teaching, the life, the promises, the kingdom, and the mystery of Jesus of Nazareth the Son of God are not proclaimed.[6]

Not only do we need to demonstrate it by our life, but we need to speak up about our faith. We should be comfortable, as Christians, to talk about who Jesus is for us, why we believe in Him, and what He did for us. We need to learn to just talk about God, instead of worrying about how we sound. The power behind the message is the Spirit of God, and we should allow Him to speak through us. God Himself converts people; we don't.

Our family can make a difference if we become attentive to every evangelistic opportunity and respond as families, realizing that the power of the Holy Spirit is at work, not our own eloquence or education. In our simplicity, God can use us. In an age of unparalleled falling away from the truth, we have been raised up by the Lord as domestic churches to carry forth the mission of the whole Church and share the gospel.

We should never forget that we are one small part of a big work that God is doing. We do not need to do it all. St. Paul wrote that one man plants and another man waters (1 Cor. 3:6–8). If we do our part to cultivate the grace already operating in an individual's life, someone else will come and finish the task. We are many parts in one body, but it is imperative that each does his or her part. Are you doing your part?

Sound the Trumpet

Now we come to the end of the journey, the final leg. Like the last lap in a five-mile race, that last burst of energy will spur us on toward the goal. You may find the end a bit surprising, but read on.

If this book has transformed your view of family life, if you have experienced a renewal of the mind, if you see family as God's plan, if you see the need for prayer, thanksgiving, work, play, sacraments, if you feel better about family life, if you believe what is said in this book—*You are hooked! You have a mission.*

Freedom comes in the confidence of knowing and doing God's will for our lives. So you ought to have experienced greater and greater freedom as you've worked through this book. God blesses us with greater knowledge. But as we know, with every blessing comes a cross. We are accountable for what we know. Paul reminded the Corinthians: "Now it is of course required of stewards that they be found trustworthy" (1 Cor. 4:2), and the Lord Himself reminds us: "Much will be required of the person entrusted with much" (Luke 12:48).

The call to action and the notion of accountability for that action is not meant to be a burden, but a great joy. We are promised blessings if we do what we are called to do. Doing is a two-way street. In order to be, we must do; in order to do, we must be. In other words, we must first be a domestic church if we are going to be missionary. On the other hand, as missionary activity is part of being church, we must do missionary work in order to be church. When we live our call, Jesus says, "Blessed are you" (John 13:17). Again the blessing comes not in the knowing, but in the doing. The word *blessing* in the Jewish language translates to "happiness" or "joy" in English. If we are blessed when we do these things, happiness and joy come in the doing. In light of the promised blessing, the action, the doing, the being on mission, although difficult, will be a tremendous joy.

And the blessings will continue. Like the early church, when we become missionary, day by day the Lord will add to our number. Look at the fruit of the early church. Christian families transformed the face of pagan Rome into the heart of the Church. Think of the possibilities for our century!

This sounds like a monumental task, but like any other task, evangelism simply involves preparation. The Scriptures tell us repeatedly that we should always be prepared to answer those who question our faith. The apostle Peter wrote, "Sanctify Christ as Lord in your hearts. Always be ready to give an explanation to anyone who asks you for a reason for your hope" (1 Peter 3:15). As a family we should always be ready. Furthermore, we should be teaching our children to be ready to share Jesus Christ as they know Him.

Smith Wigglesworth, a great Protestant evangelist and missionary, is reported to have once said, "Live ready. If you have to get ready when opportunity comes your way, you are too late. Opportunity does not wait even while you pray. You must not have to get ready; you must live ready." Do we live ready to evangelize? Are we ready to share our faith? Are we ready to tell why we have joy in our home or why our family life is peaceful?

We become more and more ready for evangelism as we practice. An athlete is ready for competition and a musician is ready for a performance only after hard work, preparation, and practice. The same principles apply in missionary activity. By living lives full of faith, hope, and love, and by preparing for daily evangelistic encounters, we can become an example of church in the world. Today many families are overwhelmed by the circumstances of the age. We have been placed in the midst of the world to be a hope, to be a sign, to be a sacrament that shows forth the love of God.

Conclusion

The Domestic Church in the Modern World

All authority in heaven and on earth has been given to me. Therefore go and make disciples of all nations, baptizing them in the name of the Father and of the Son and of the Holy Spirit, and teaching them to obey everything I have commanded you. And surely I am with you always, to the very end of the age. (Matt. 28:18 NIV)

The passage above is referred to by most evangelical Christians as the Great Commission. To whom is the Lord talking? The answer is obvious, isn't it? He is talking to you and me. But He is not talking only to us as individuals. He did not create us only to be individuals. He created us to be a people and He positioned us in families. The mission of the Church in the modern world is the mission of the Church in every generation, to make disciples. The Church in every generation has risen to the challenge of that generation, and so will she in the twenty-first century. However, we need to understand a basic principle of evangelical Christian mission.

I identify very much with being an evangelical Christian. In my book *Evangelical Catholics*,[1] I define an evangelical Christian as one who is in love with Jesus and committed to making the gospel known. I argue throughout that entire book that *evangelical* is an adjective. It is. It's an adjective that should not even need to be used to describe a Christian. All Christians should be on fire to make the gospel known. All Christian families should be likewise. But unfortunately that is all too often not the case. Yet, when a Christian or a Christian family is living and demonstrating the gospel, they are a powerful tool in the hands of the Lord. Just as evangelization doesn't usually begin with whole nations converting, but with individuals, so too the Church will not be revived corporately en masse. Rather, her individual cells, her families, will be restored one by one. One domestic church linking arms with another domestic church, bringing renewal to the entire extended family. This is what the Church is all about. The extended family of those who belong to Jesus Christ is called to change the world.

We enter into the twenty-first century facing tremendous challenges. Many tell us we are in a post-Christian age. Yet it is an exciting time to be alive. Paralleled perhaps only by the first century of the Christian church. It too faced a predominately pagan world and turned it on its head. Actually it turned it on its knees. So must we.

On the verge of this new millennium of Christianity, we are challenged to put forth the same solution that our first-century predecessors did. That solution is a person named Jesus, who is God's answer to a fallen human race. We are called to transform all things through Him. Remember, a little leaven does indeed go a long way, and a tiny mustard seed produces a huge tree. Because the first twelve disciples and then the seventy-two took the Lord at His word and lived committed lives, not only individually but in their families, the Roman Empire was converted and the world was transformed. It can still be done. It must be done. The choice is ours and it begins behind the front door.

The Christian family is the hope for the next century. We are living in an age of increasing disregard for God and the things of God. However, as Father John Catoir says, "It is better to light one candle than to curse the darkness." That one candle should be our own family. I have tried to lay out in this book a vision for a transformed Christian family life. But the vision is not mine. I pray it is the Lord's. The blueprint is simply found in His word and it has been repeatedly proclaimed by His church. The blueprint is as relevant today as ever and perhaps even more desperately needed. While contemporary verbal, social, legal, and political engineers seek to redefine family, the Christian family must reclaim its heritage and present it as a gift to the world. Certainly the solution to the current state of affairs in the world is a revival in the Church so that she can spread the saving message of the gospel to the nations. However, a revival in the Church must first begin at home.

Several years ago I had the distinct privilege of bringing Richard John Neuhaus to the Franciscan University of Steubenville where I served as Dean of Evangelism for a number of years. We wanted to honor Pastor Neuhaus for his marvelous work in challenging contemporary Christians to take their faith into the marketplace. Accompanying me on the journey was a dear friend. We all stopped for lunch. My friend opined for at least thirty minutes about the desperate state of the contemporary world. By the time he was through I felt depressed. Pastor Neuhaus, having years of wisdom on both of us looked us both in the eye and said, "These may be difficult times, but these are *our* times. We were born for times such as these. Don't ever forget the predominant virtue of the Christian life is hope. The gospel is a gospel of hope."

The message of this book is one of hope. It is good news. Your family and mine, through God's grace, is a domestic church. Let's begin to live like one and watch the transformation. First of ourselves, then our neighborhoods, our parishes, our congregations, our denominations, and ultimately our nation and the world. Then we will rejoice with the countless millions of those who have gone on before us.

The kingdom of the world has become the kingdom of our Lord and of his Christ, and he will reign for ever and ever (Rev. 11:15).

NOTES

Chapter 1
1. Austin Flannery, O.P., ed., "Lumen Gentium," *The Documents of Vatican II: The Conciliar and Post Conciliar Documents,* (Grand Rapids, MI: William B. Eerdmans Publishing, 1987), par. 13.

Chapter 2
1. Henri Blocher, *In the Beginning* (Downers Grove, IL: InterVarsity Press, 1984), 86.

Chapter 3
1. John Paul II, *The Lay Members of Christ's Faithful People* (Boston: Daughters of St. Paul, 1988), par. 59.

Chapter 4
1. C. S. Lewis, *The Weight of Glory and Other Addresses* (Grand Rapids, MI: William B. Eerdmans, 1949), 13-14.
2. Ibid., 15.
3. Austin Flannery, O.P., ed., "Lumen Gentium," *The Documents of Vatican II: The Conciliar and Post Conciliar Documents,* (Grand Rapids, MI: William B. Eerdmans Publishing, 1987), par. 39.
4. Thomas Howard, *Hallowed Be This House* (San Francisco: Ignatius Press, 1979), 13.

Chapter 5
1. Bishop Fulton John Sheen, *Treasure in Clay: The Autobiography of Fulton J. Sheen* (Garden City, NY: Doubleday, 1980), 334.
2. Ibid., 339.

Chapter 6
1. Francis de Sales, *Introduction to the Devout Life,* trans. by John K. Ryan, (New York: Doubleday, 1989), 40-41.
2. Ibid., 43-44.
3. Aristotle, quoted by de Sales in *Introduction to the Devout Life,* 40-41.

Chapter 7

1. John Paul II, *The Role of the Christian Family in the Modern World* (Boston: Daughters of St. Paul, 1981), par. 38.

2. Andrew Murray, *How To Raise Your Children for Christ* (Minneapolis, MN: Bethany House Pub., 1975), 96.

3. Ibid., 96–97.

4. James Dobson, *Dr. Dobson Answers Your Questions* (Wheaton, IL: Tyndale House Publishers, 1983), 42.

5. Also see Murray, 122–127.

6. *John Paul II in America* (Boston: Daughters of St. Paul, 1980), par. 4, 135.

7. Dobson, 43.

8. Jerome once said that "Ignorance of the Scripture is ignorance of Christ." From the prologue of the commentary on Isaiah by Jerome the priest. Sept. 30 in the *Liturgy of Hours* (New York: Catholic Book Publishing Co., 1975).

9. Murray, 260.

Chapter 8

1. John Wesley, "On Family Religion," *A Compendium of Wesley's Theology,* ed. by Robert Burtner and Robert Chiles (New York: Abingdon, 1954), 239.

2. Austin Flannery, O.P., ed., "Lumen Gentium," *The Documents of Vatican II: The Conciliar and Post Conciliar Documents,* (Grand Rapids, MI: William B. Eerdmans Publishing, 1987), par. 30.

3. James Dobson, *Dr. Dobson Answers Your Questions* (Wheaton, IL: Tyndale House Publishers, 1983), 129.

4. Ibid., 123.

5. Andrew Murray, *How to Raise Your Children for Christ,* (Minneapolis, MN: Bethany House Publishers, 1975), 129, 131.

Chapter 9

1. Michael Scanlan, T.O.R., and Ann T. Shields, *And Their Eyes Were Opened* (Ann Arbor, MI: Servant Publications, 1975) 15.

2. Ibid., 30, 38.

3. Austin Flannery, O.P., ed., "Lumen Gentium," *The Documents of Vatican II: The Conciliar and Post Conciliar Documents,* (Grand Rapids, MI: William B. Eerdmans Publishing, 1987), par. 11.

4. Thomas Howard, *Hallowed Be This House* (San Francisco: Ignatius Press, 1979), 66–68.

Chapter 10

1. John Paul II, *The Role of the Christian Family in the Modern World* (Boston: Daughters of St. Paul, 1981), par. 62.

2. *John Paul II, in America* (Boston: Daughters of St. Paul, 1980).

3. Ibid., 138

4. Michael Hennel, "Evangelical Spirituality," in *The Westminster Dictionary of Christian Spirituality,* ed. by Gordon S. Wakefield (Philadelphia: The Westminster Press, 1983), 138.

5. John Paul II, *The Role of the Christian Family in the Modern World,* par. 59,

6. Ibid.

Chapter 12

1. John Paul II, *On Human Work,* (Washington, D.C.: United States Catholic Conference, 1981), 1.

2. William Barclay, *Ethics in a Permissive Society* (New York: Harper & Roe, 1971), 94; Charles Colson and Jack Eckerd, *Why America Doesn't Work* (Dallas: Word Publishing, 1991), 33.

3. For a wonderful treatment on the "roots of work" see, Charles Colson and Jack Eckerd, *Why America Doesn't Work* (Dallas: Word Publishing, 1991), 31–40.

4. Ibid.

Chapter 13

1. Robert Lee, quoting Irenaeus, *Religion and Leisure in America,* (New York: Abingdon Press, 1964), 35.

2. Robert Johnston, *The Christian at Play,* (Grand Rapids, MI: William B. Eerdmans Publishing, 1983), 34.

3. Ibid., 92.

4. Joseph Pieper, *Leisure: The Basis of Culture,* trans. by Alexander Dru, (New York: Random House, 1963), 21.

Chapter 14

1. Austin Flannery, O.P., ed., "Church in the Modern World," *The Documents of Vatican II: The Conciliar and Post Conciliar Documents,* (Grand Rapids, MI: William B. Eerdmans Publishing, 1987).

2. John Paul II, *The Lay Members of Christ's Faithful People* (Boston: Daughters of St. Paul, 1988), par. 3.

3. Michael Waldstein, "Laborers in the Lord's Vineyard: The Church Becomes Present in Life," Aug. 1990, lecture at Franciscan University, Steubenville, OH.

4. Henri De Lubac, *Splendour of the Church*, trans. by Michael Mason, (Glen Rock, NJ: Paulist Press, 1963), 130–31.

5. Ibid., 131.

6. Bishop Augustine, sermon 96, *Liturgy of the Hours* (New York: Catholic Book Publishing Co., 1975), vol. 4, 1828; cf. *Pseudo-Chrysostom, Opus Imperfectum in Mattheum*, hom. 23 (56, 755).

7. Augustine, as quoted by De Lubac in *The Splendour of the Church*, 120.

Chapter 15

1. Paul VI, *Evangelization in the Modern World*, par. 71.

2. John Paul II, *The Lay Members of Christ's Faithful People* (Boston: Daughters of St. Paul, 1988); *The Role of the Christian Family in the Modern World* (Boston: Daughters of St. Paul, 1981), par. 85.

3. Bishop John Chrysostom, homily 20, *Liturgy of the Hours* (New York: Catholic Book Publishing Co., 1975), 1826–1827.

4. *John Paul II in America* (Boston: Daughters of St. Paul, 1980), no. 4.

5. *Evangelization in the Modern World*, par. 71.

6. Ibid., par. 22.

Conclusion

1. Keith Fournier, *Evangelical Catholics* (Nashville: Thomas Nelson Publishers, 1990).

ABOUT THE AUTHOR

Keith A. Fournier and his wife, Laurine, live in Chesapeake, Virginia. They are the proud parents of five very normal children ranging in age from three to fifteen. He is a practicing attorney and currently serves as the Executive Director of the American Center for Law and Justice in Virginia Beach, Virginia. The Center is a public interest law firm engaged in pro-liberty, pro-life, and pro-family causes. It is located at the CBN Center and was founded by Pat Robertson. He formerly served as General Counsel and Dean of Evangelism at the Franciscan University in Steubenville, Ohio.

A published author, Keith has written *Will the Real Jesus Please Stand, Titles of the Holy Spirit,* and *Evangelical Catholics.*

He is the host of the popular family life series on the Eternal Word Television Network entitled, "The Domestic Church." The former host of the radio program "Purpose for Living," he currently hosts "Law & Justice: Reclaiming Liberty, Life and the Family," heard over the CBN Radio Network.